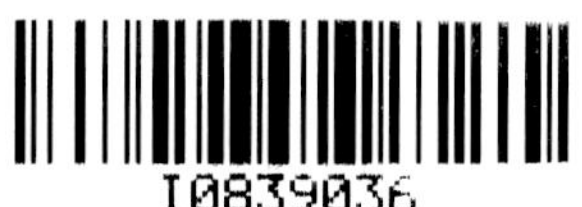

Coloring book for adults and kids amazing elephant image for design

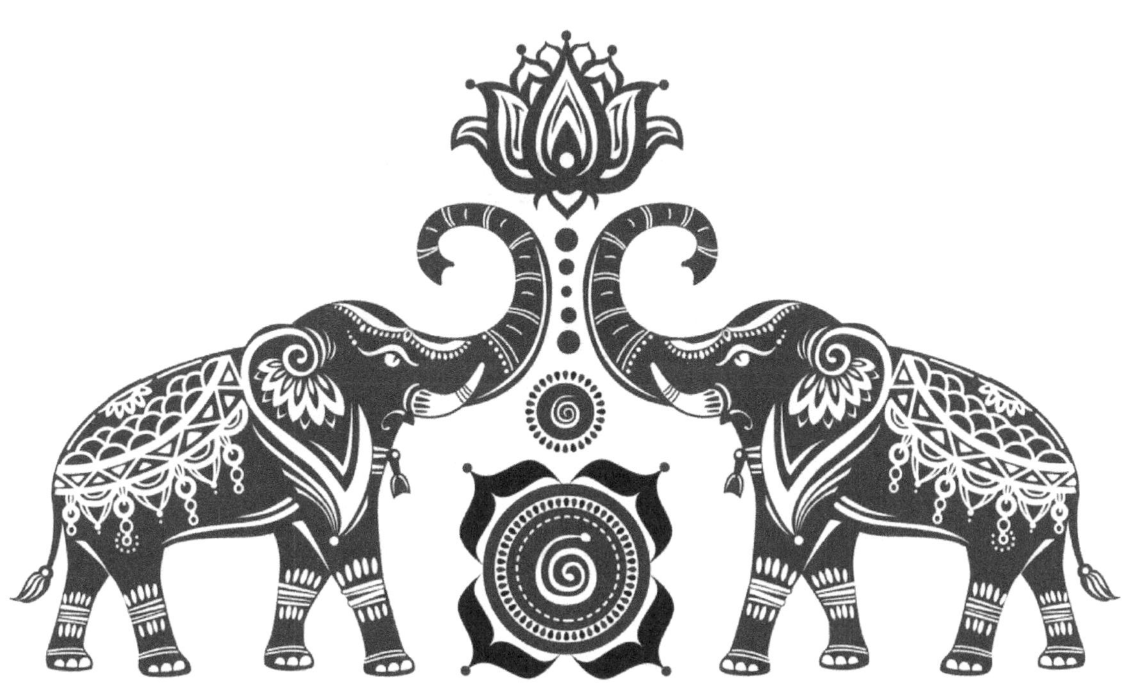

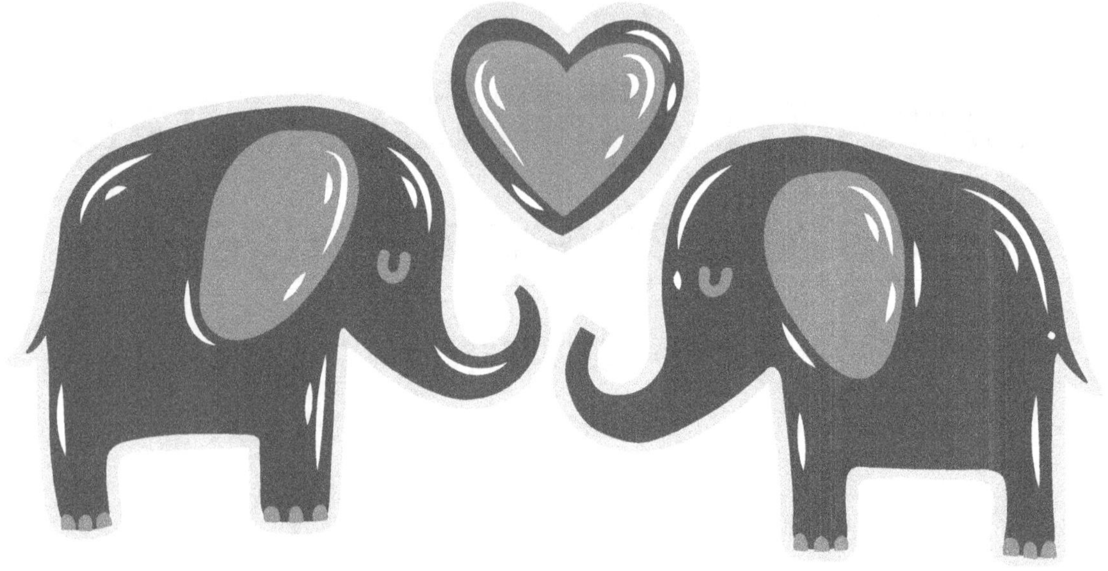

This coloring book is
belongs to

--.

--.

--.

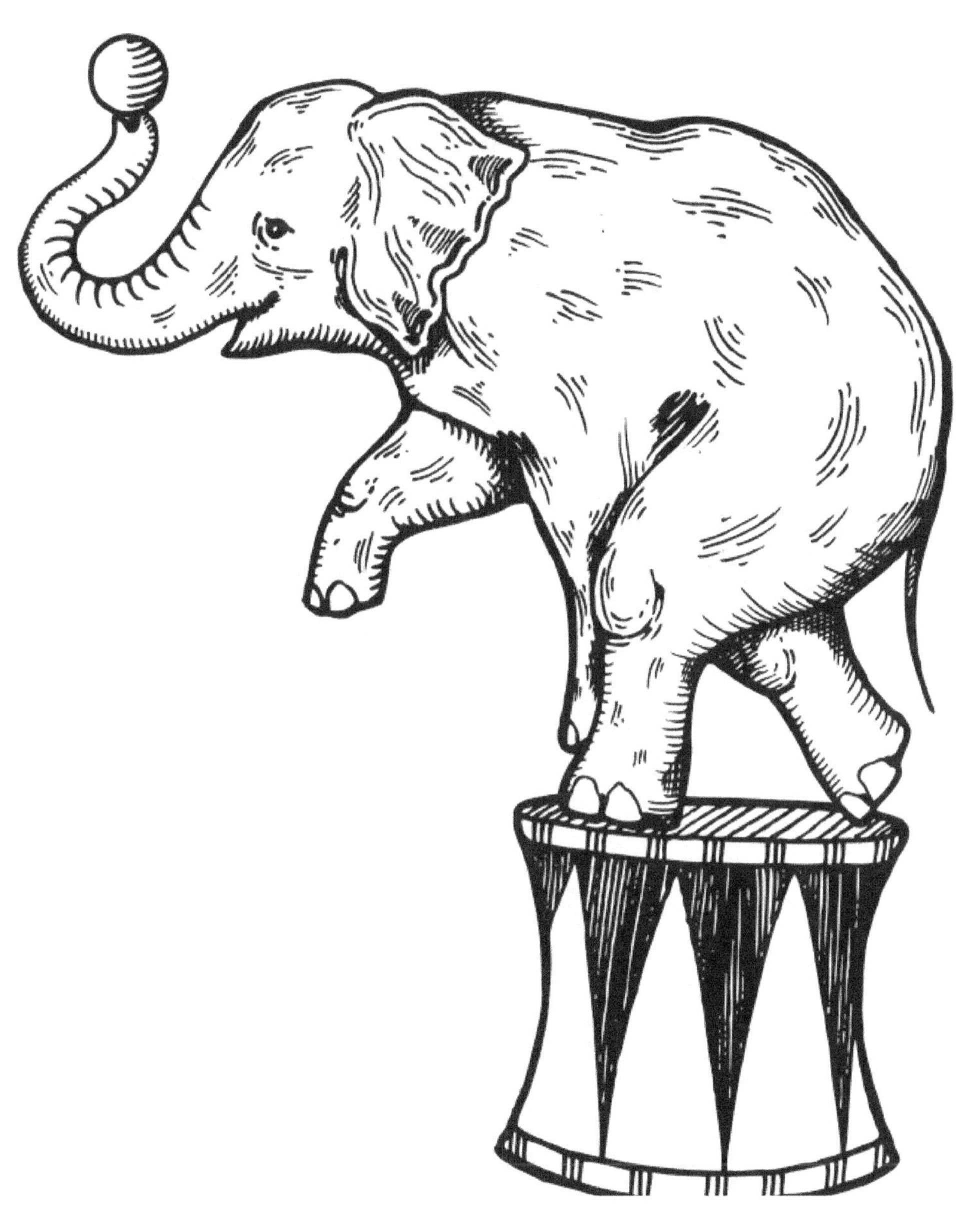

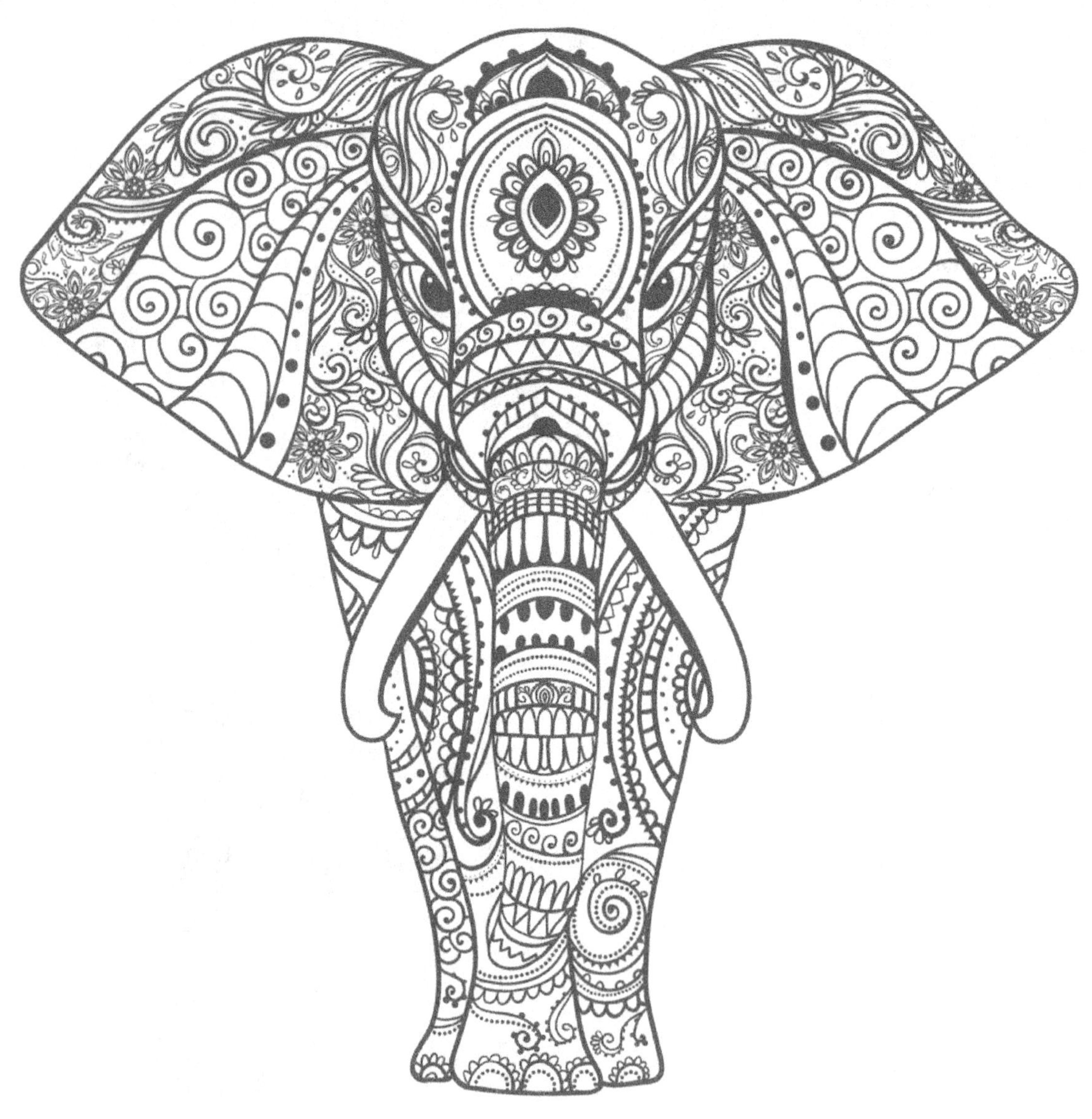

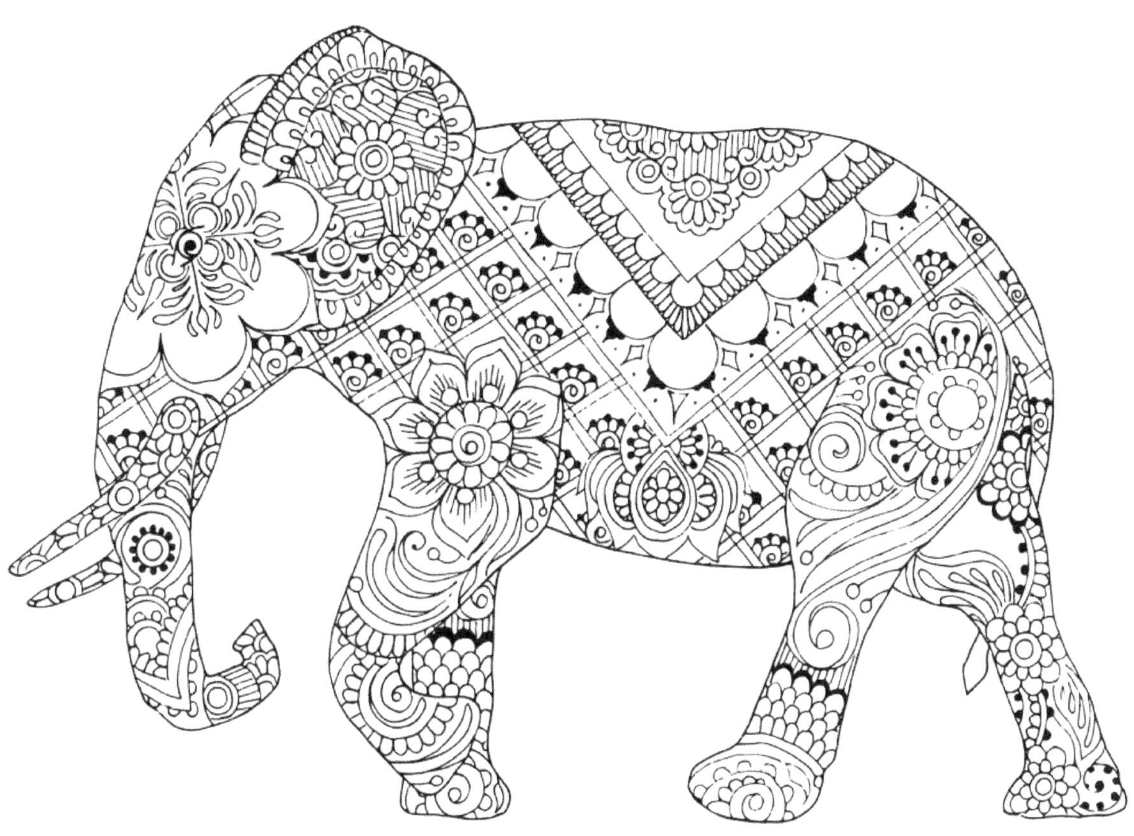

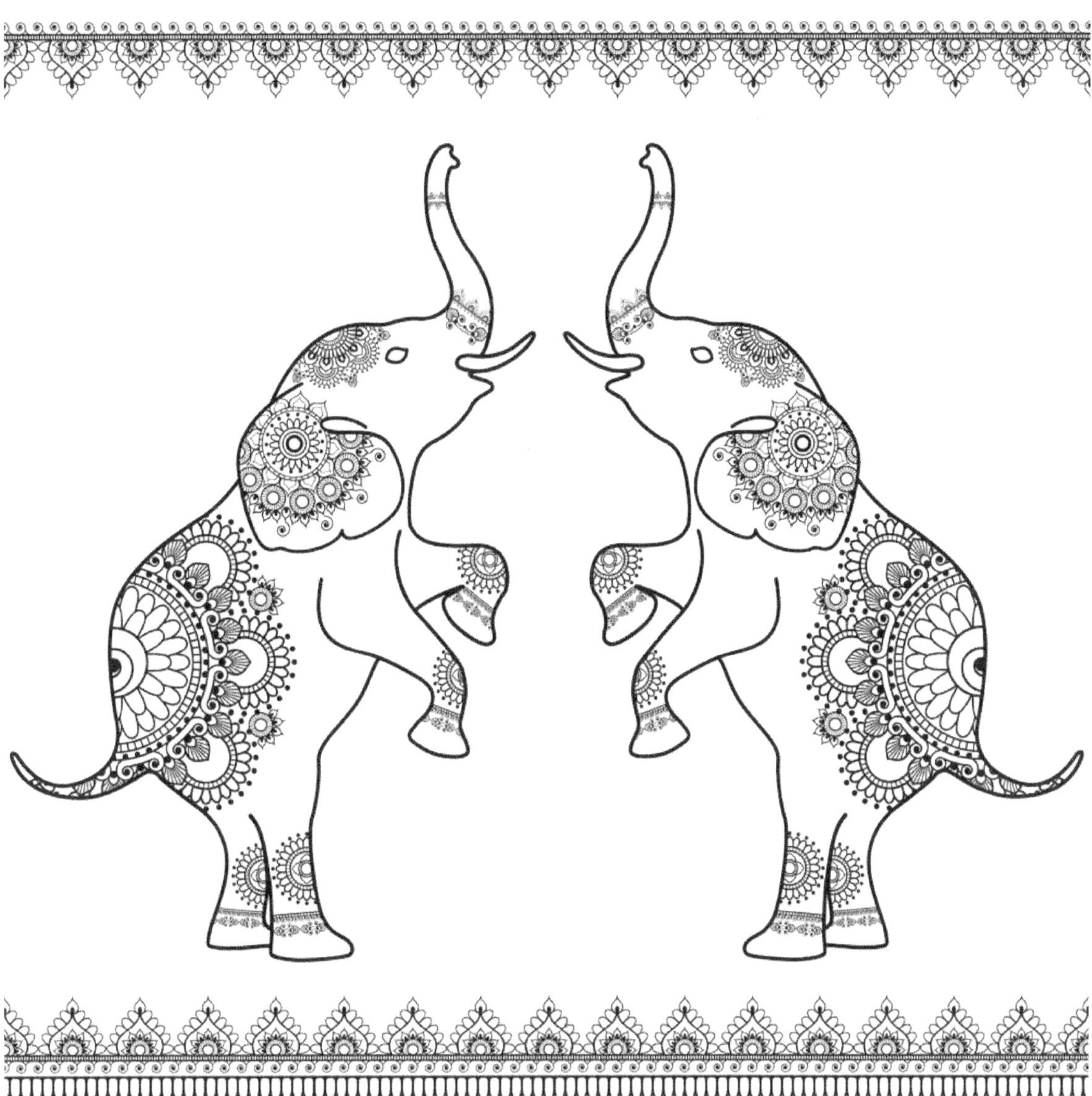

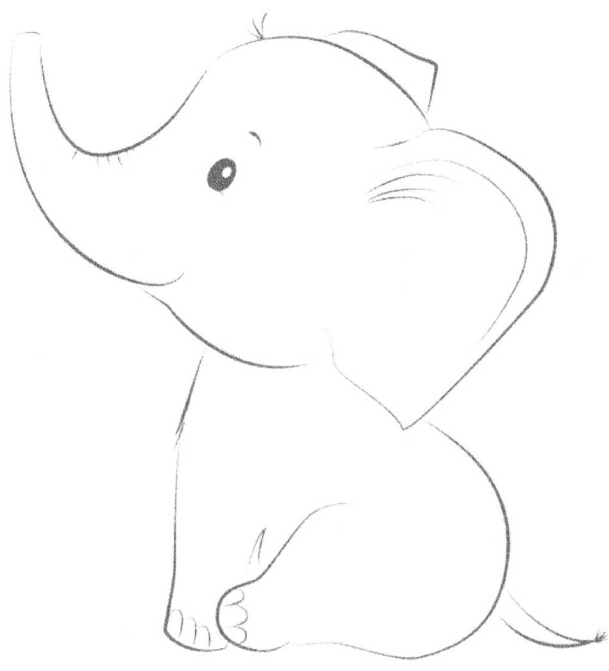

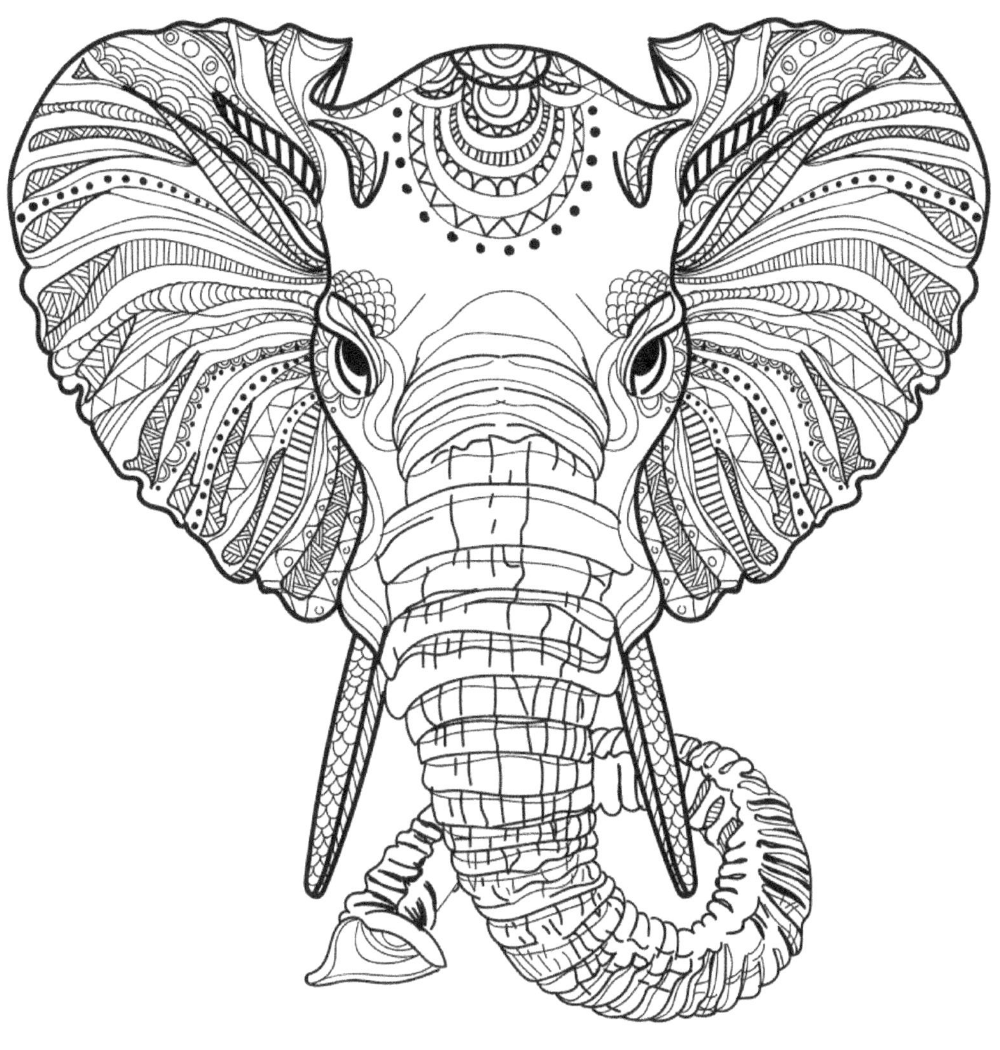

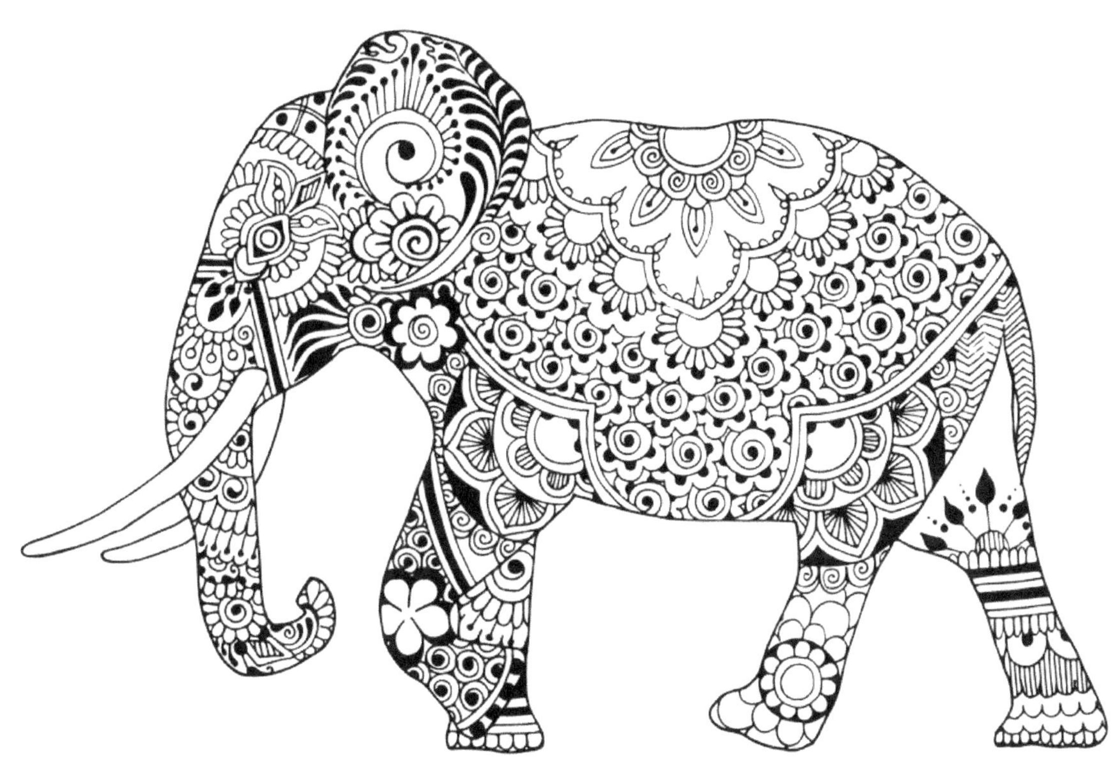

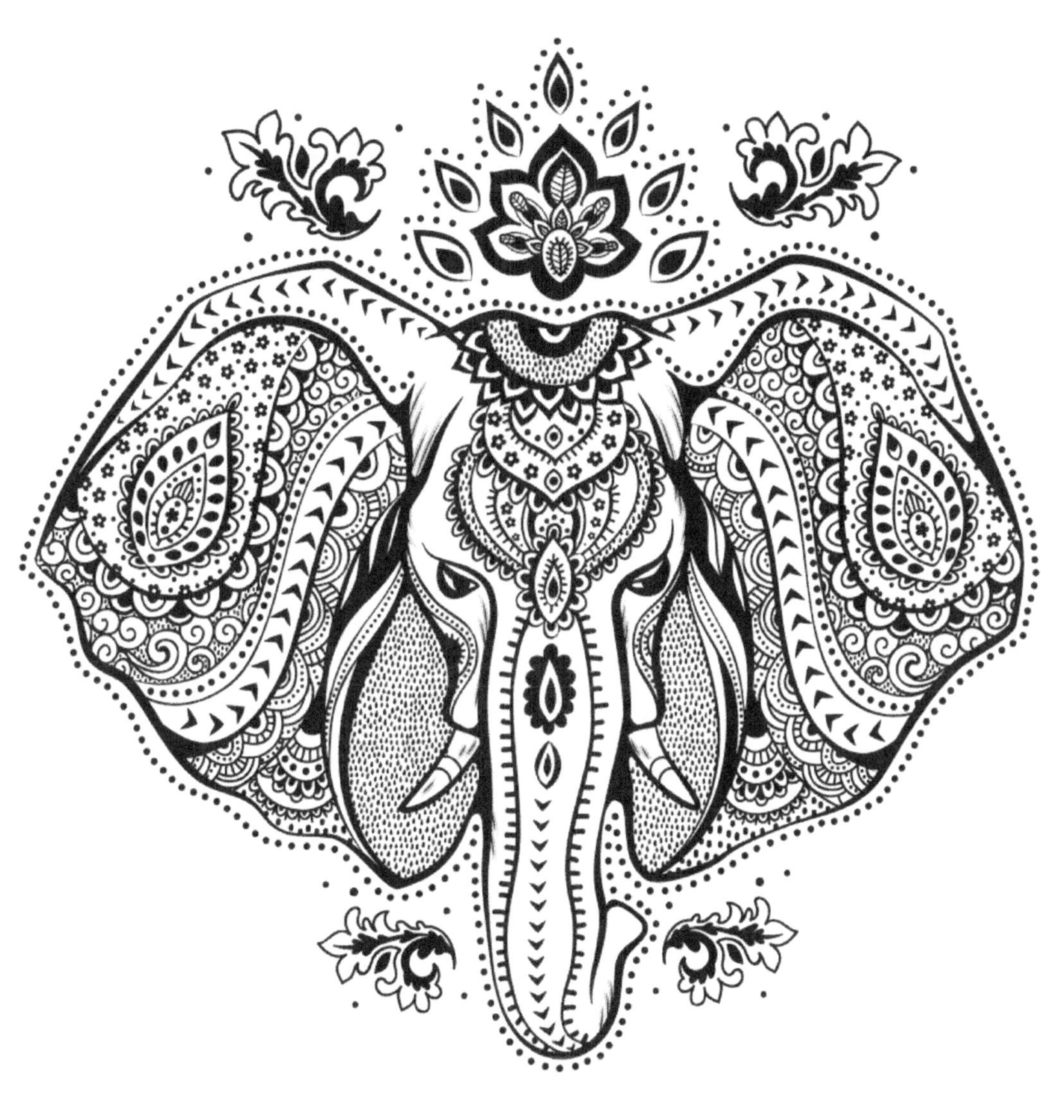

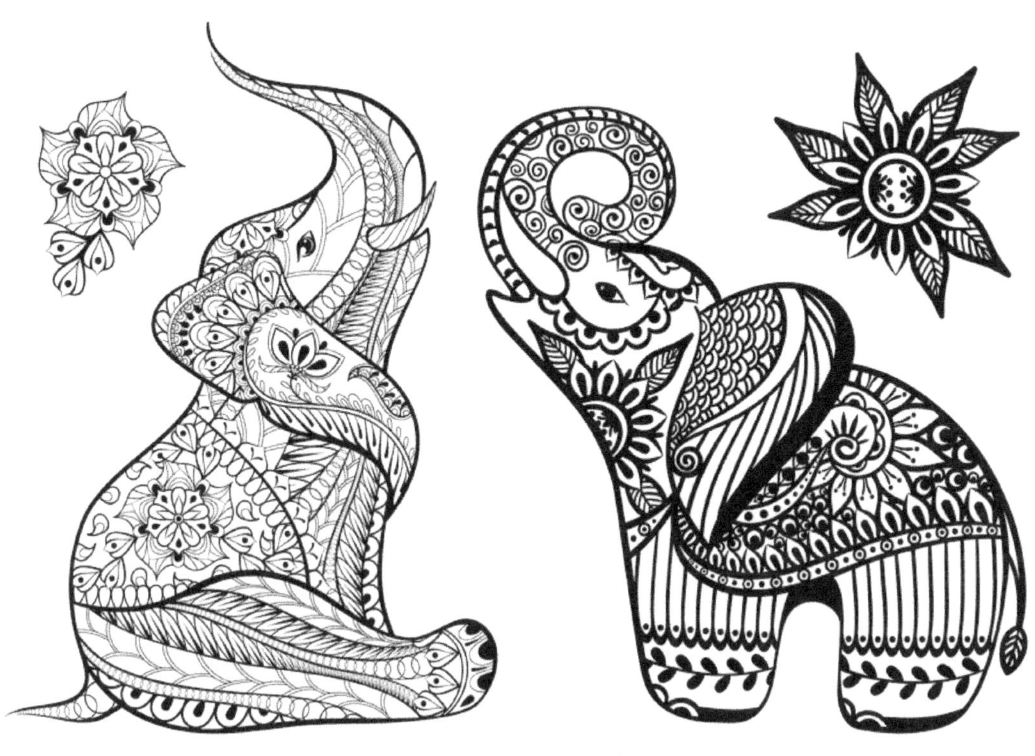

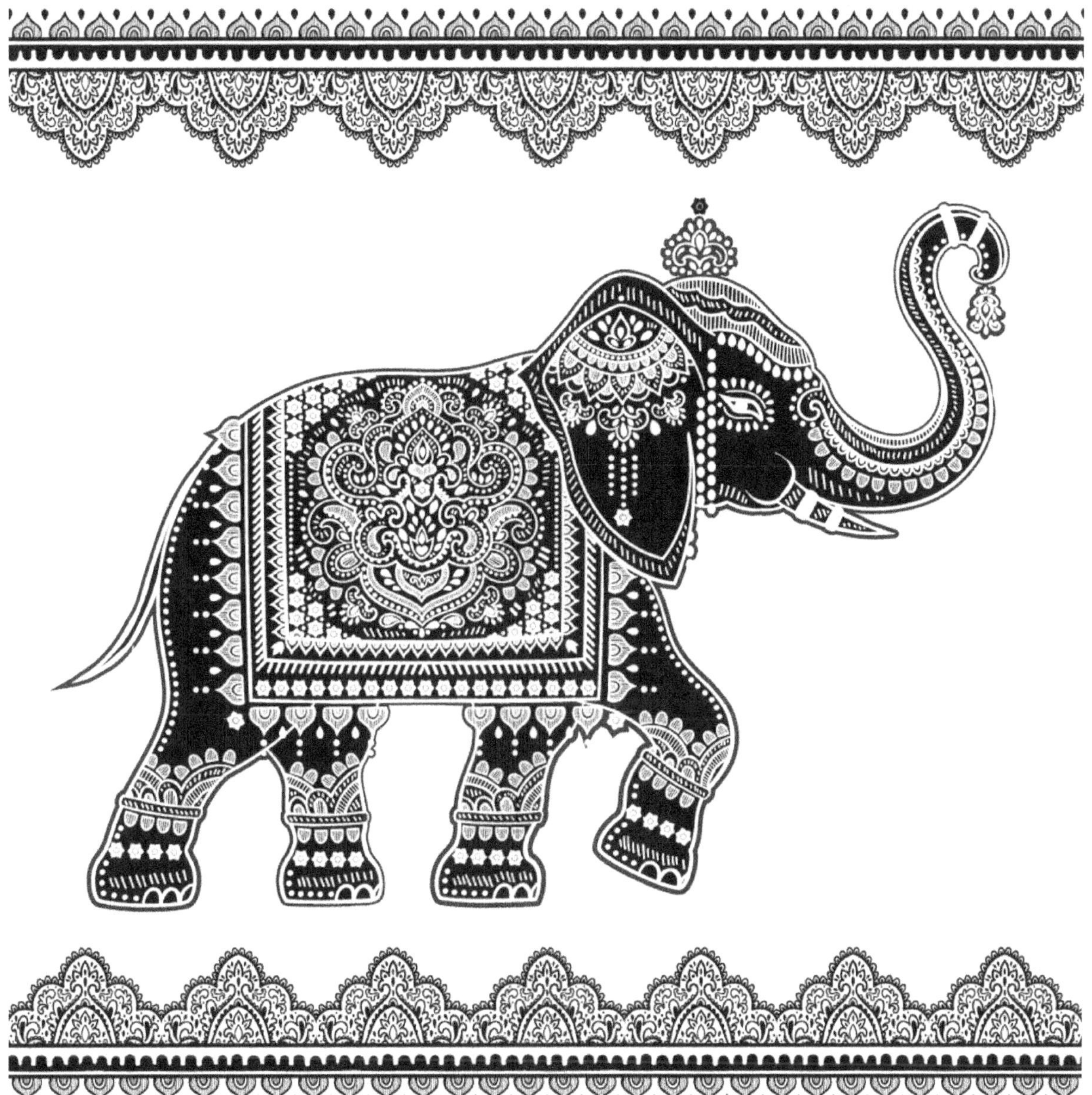

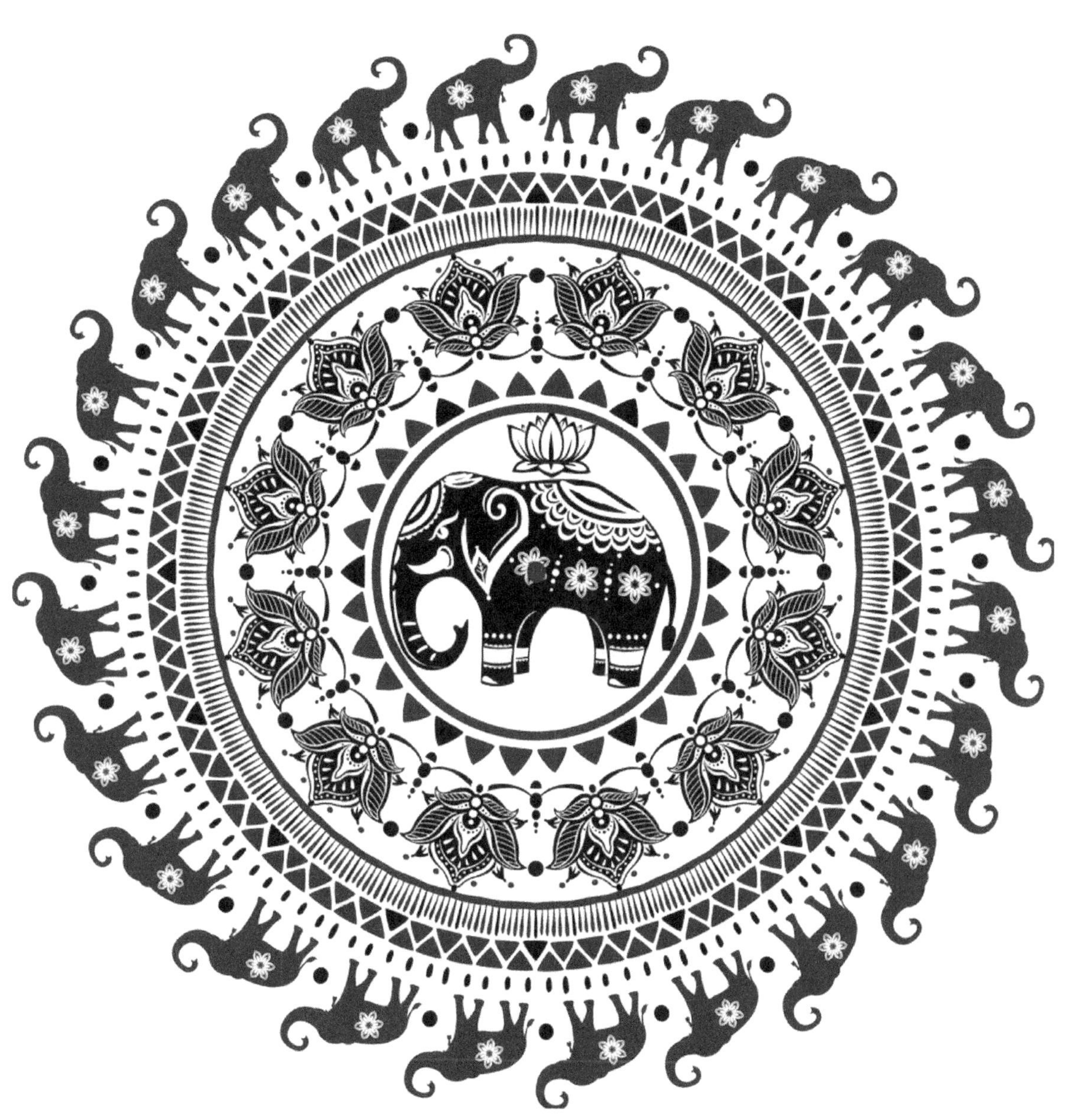

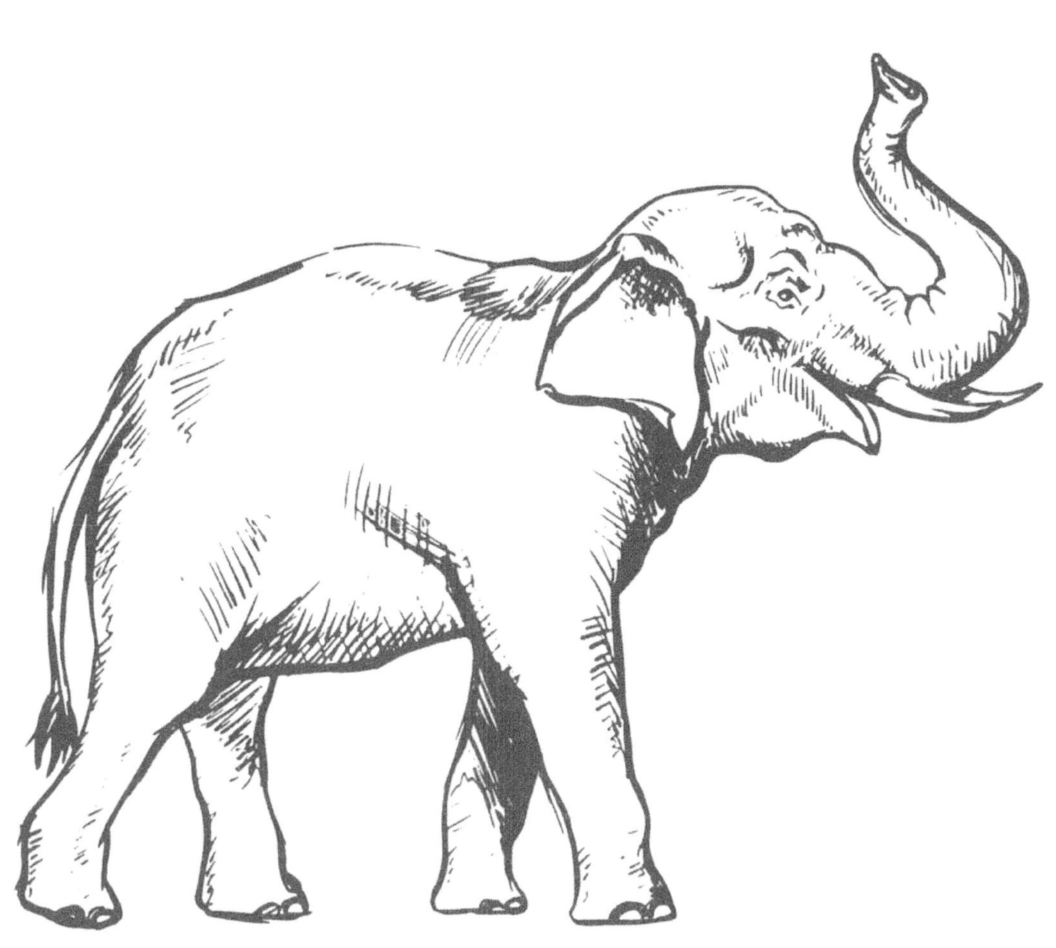

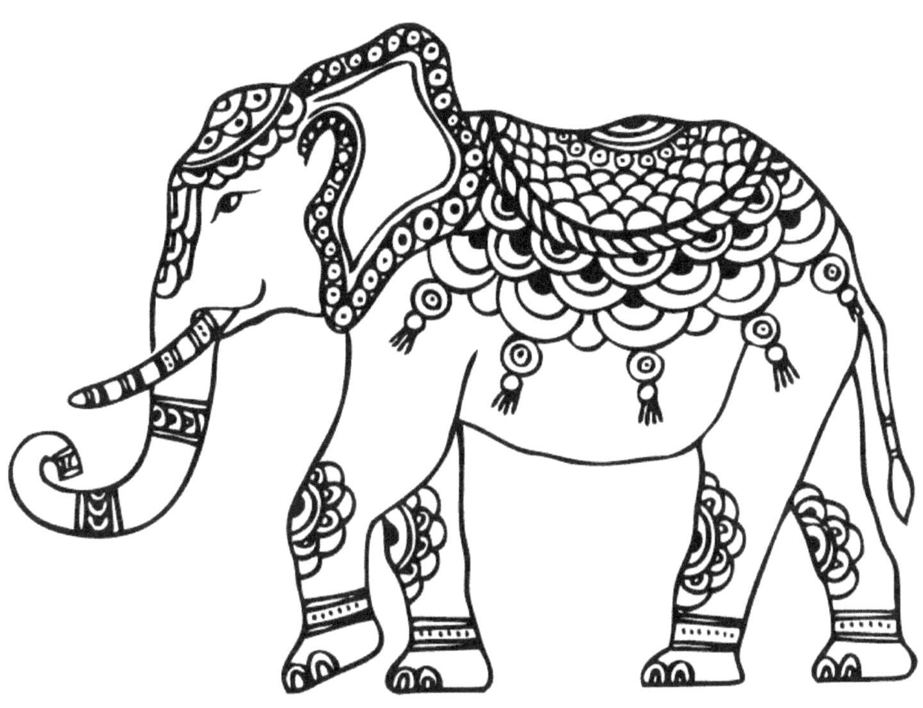

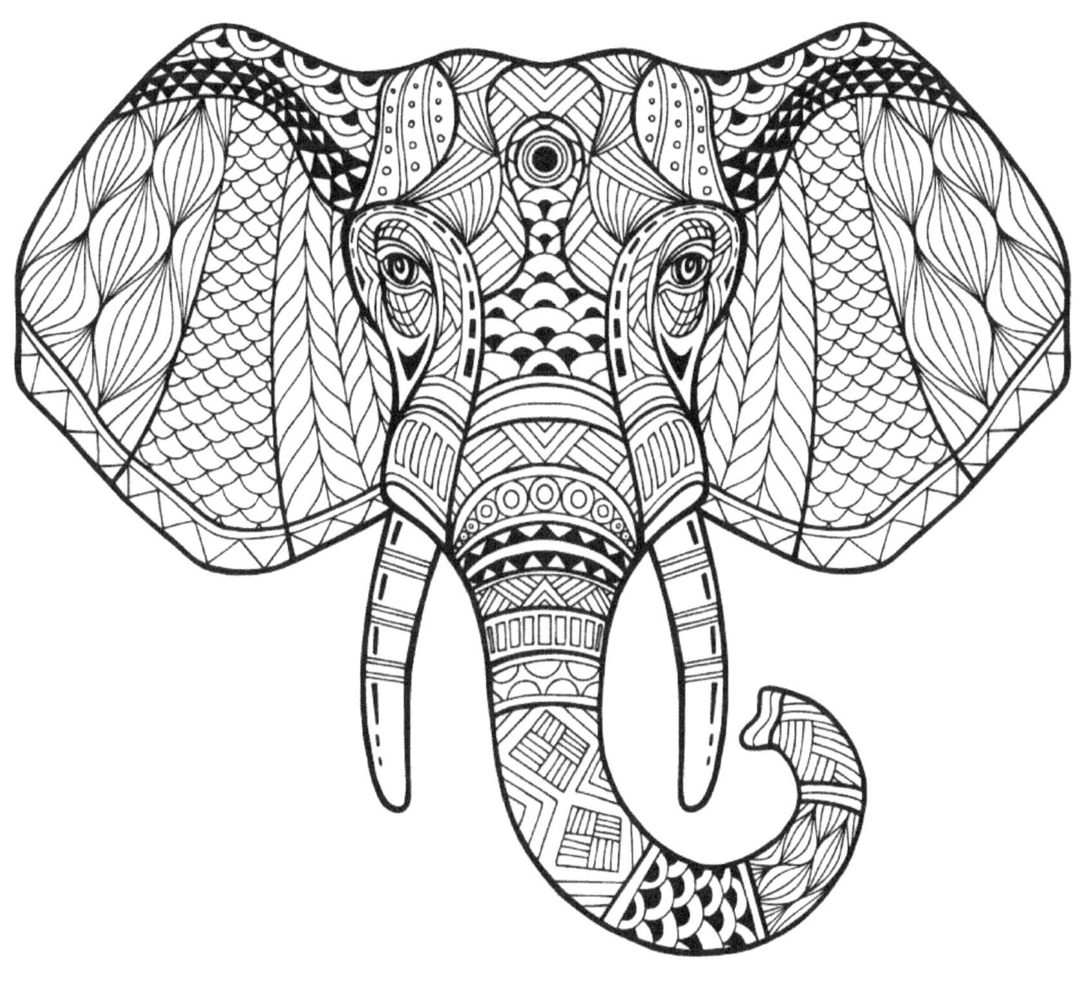

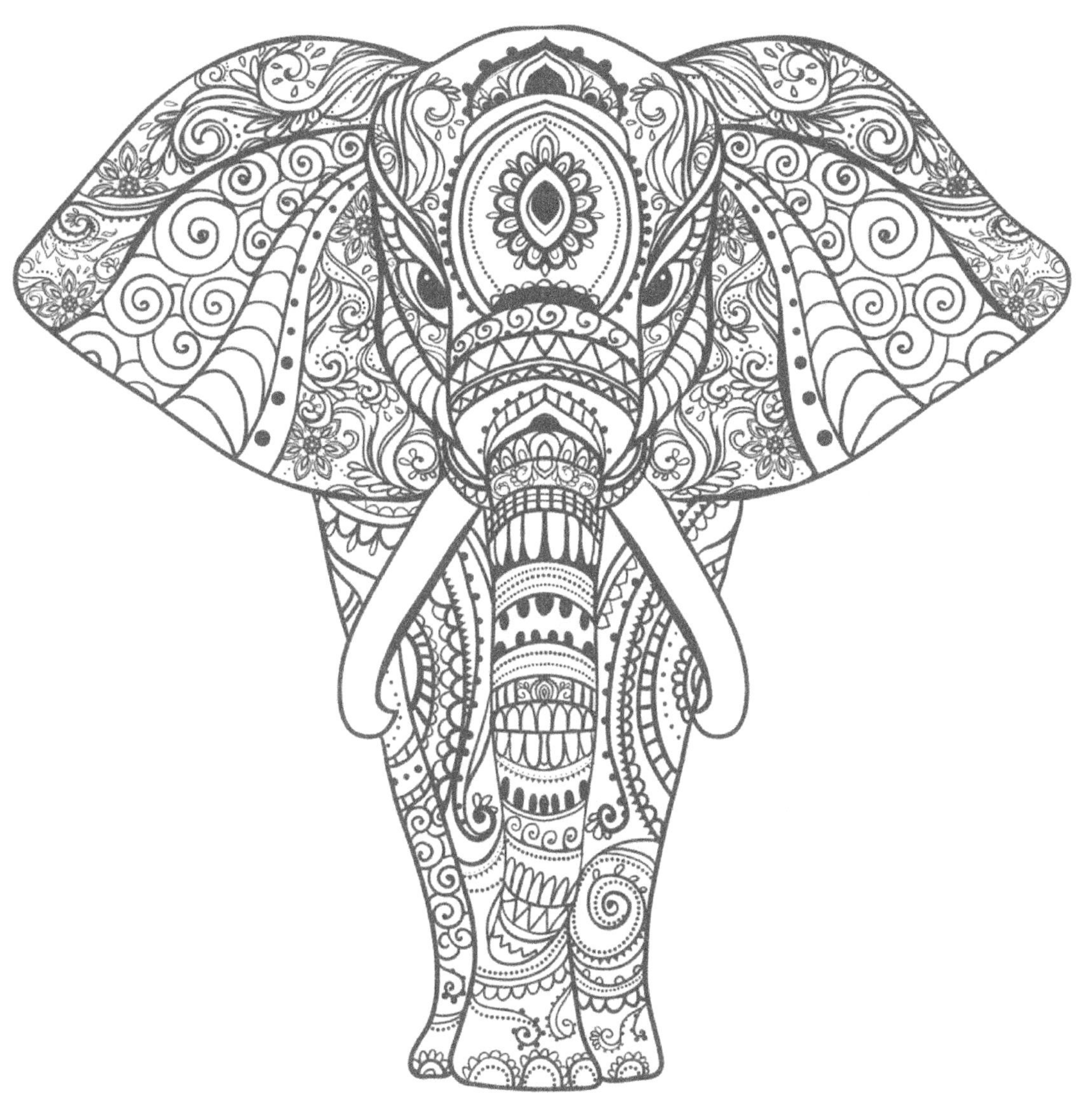

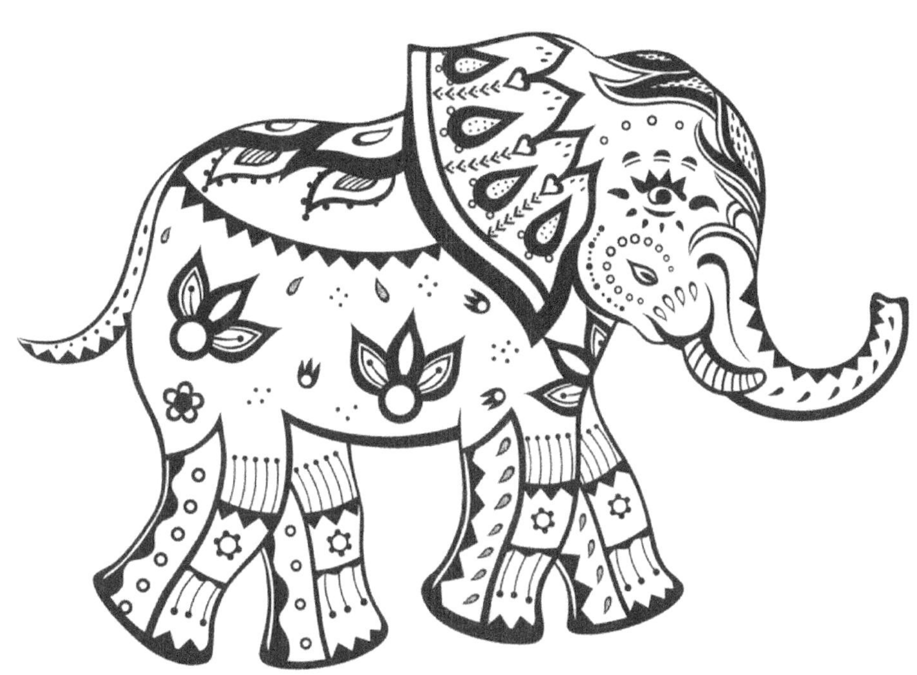

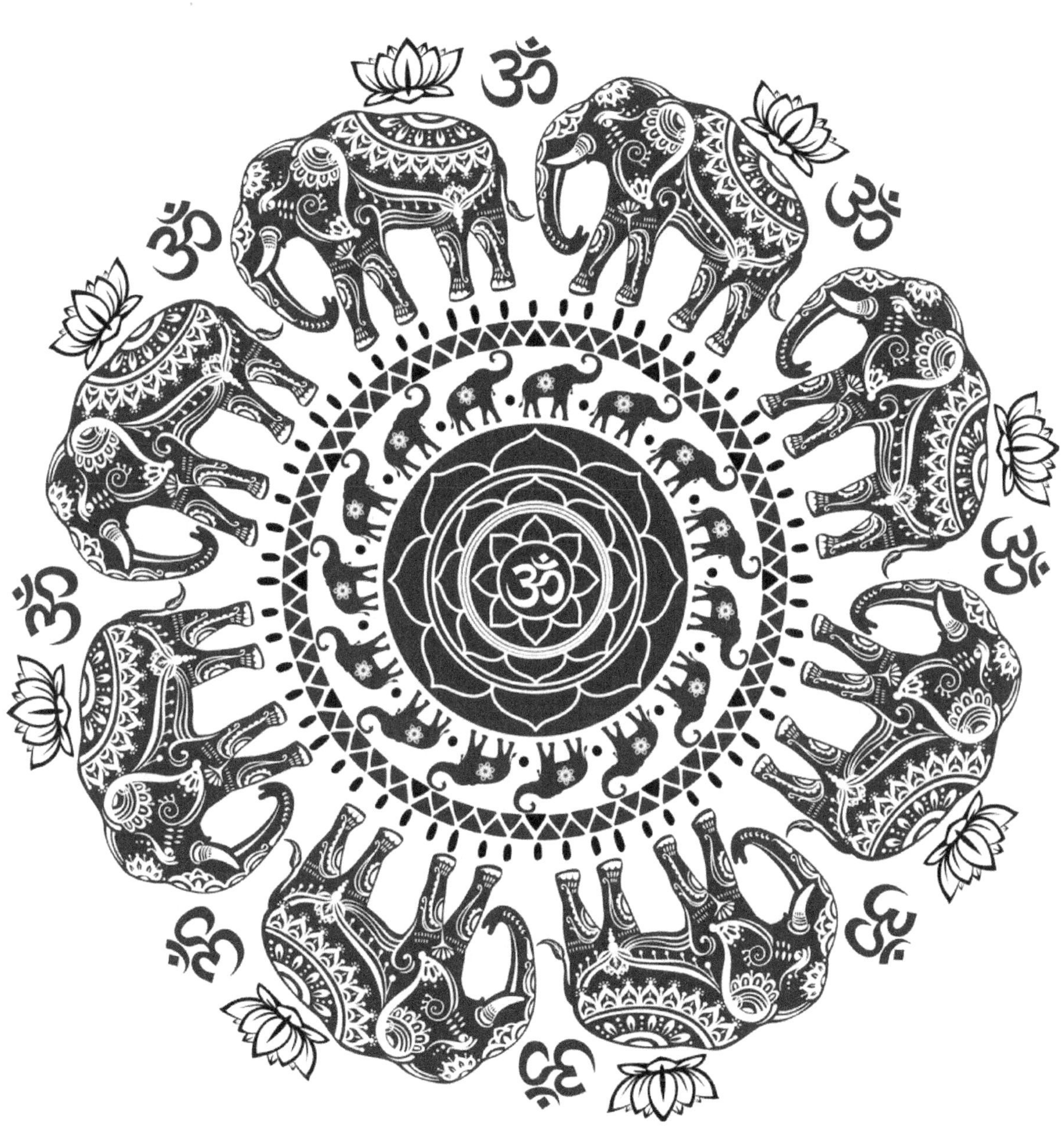

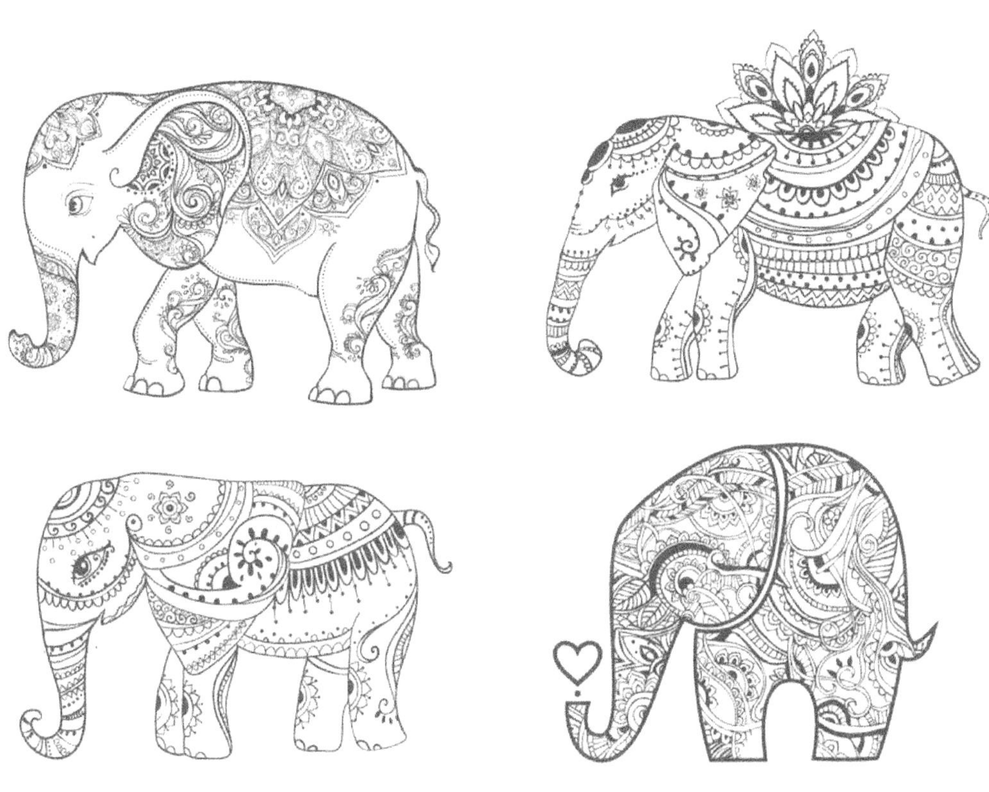

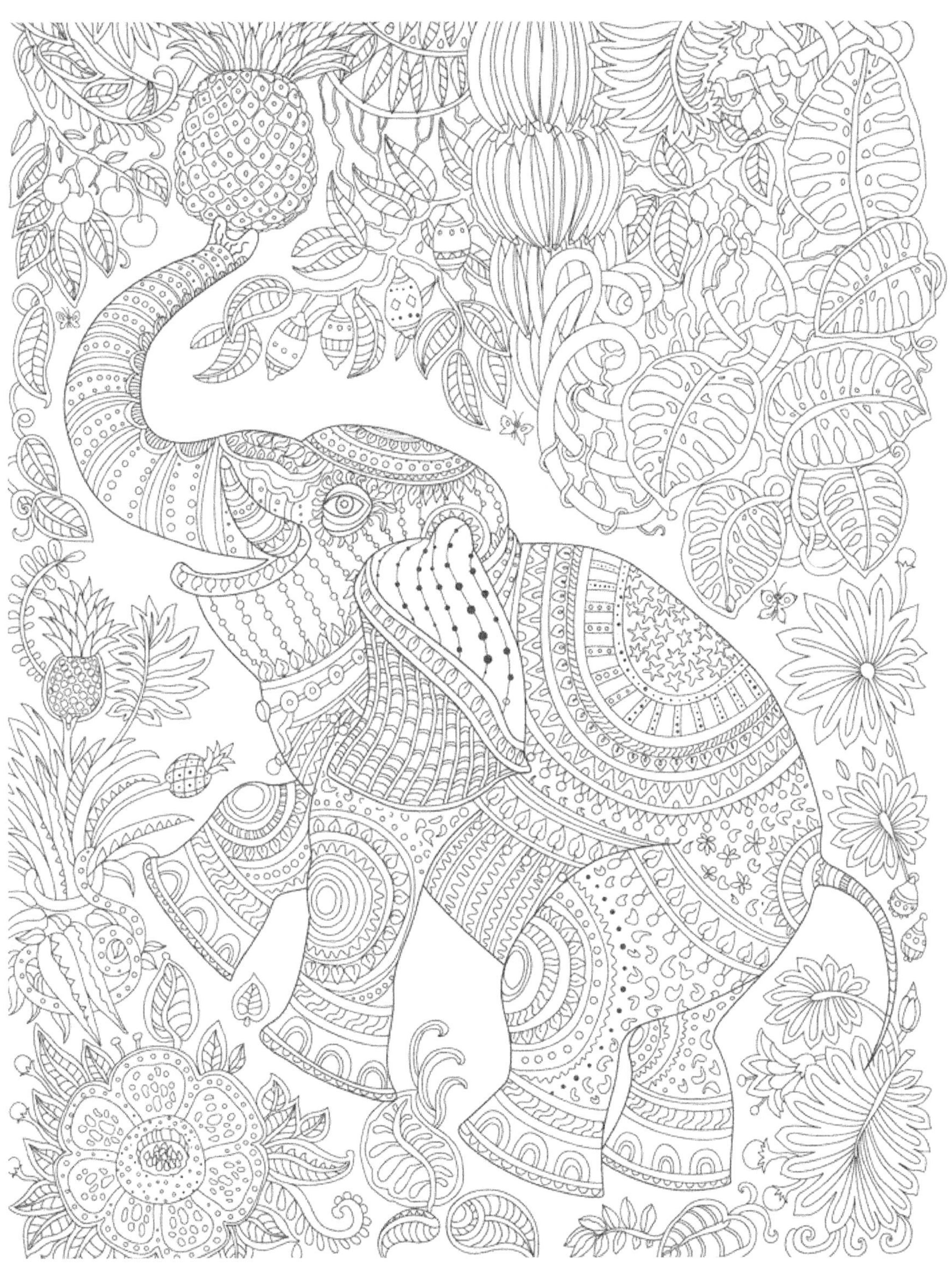

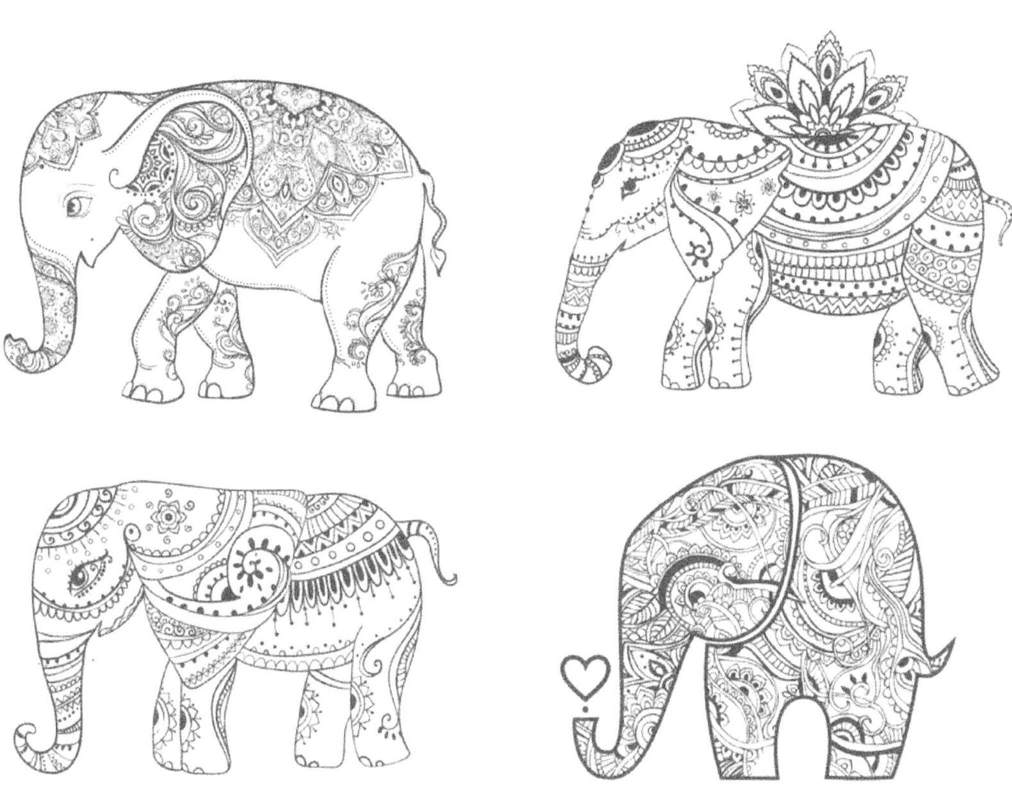

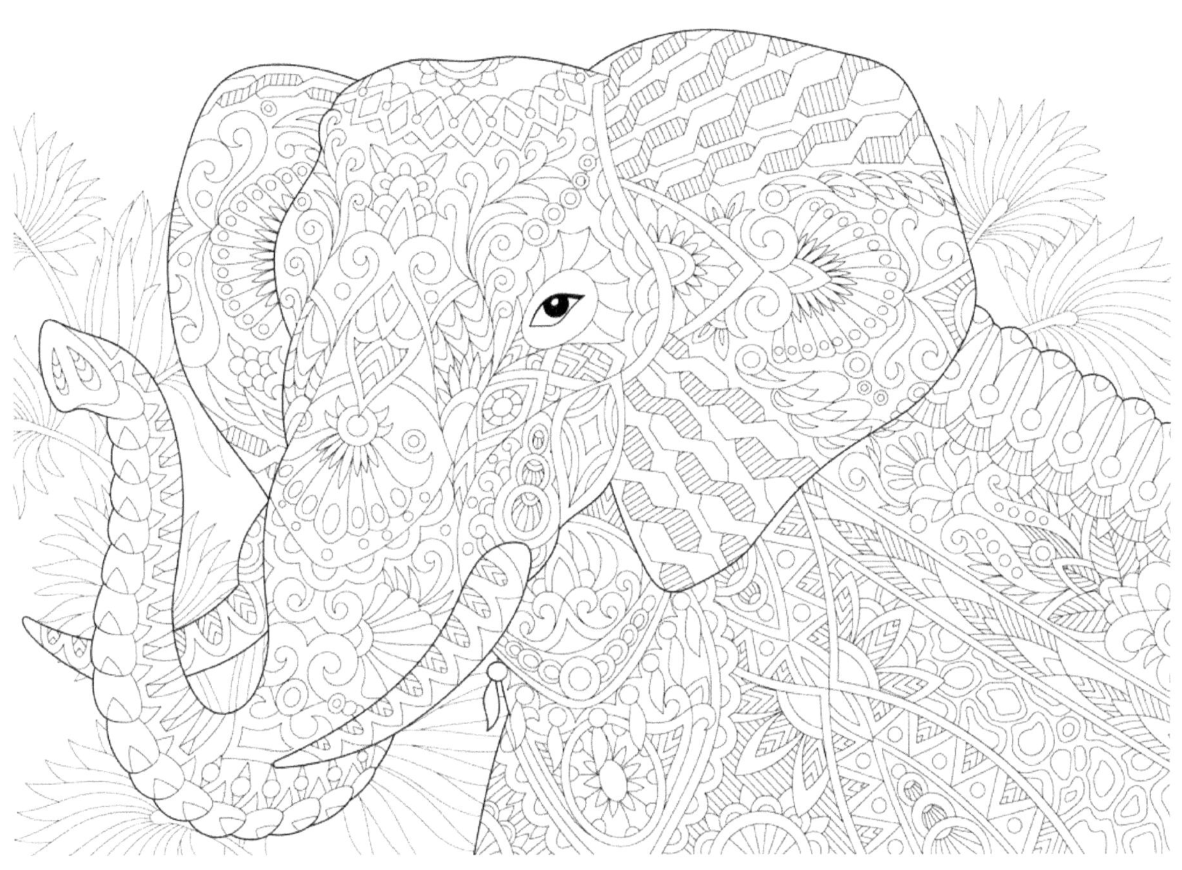

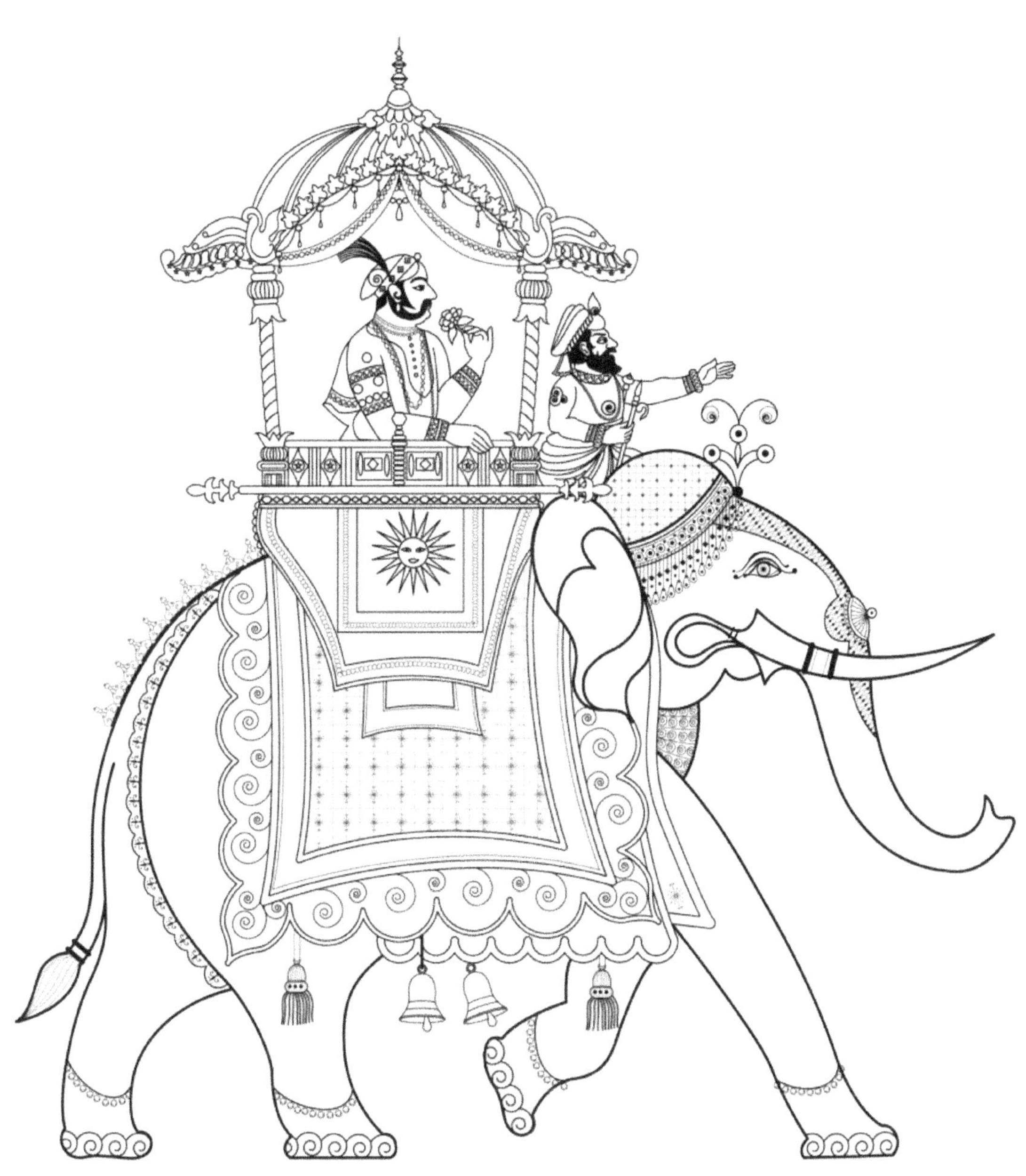

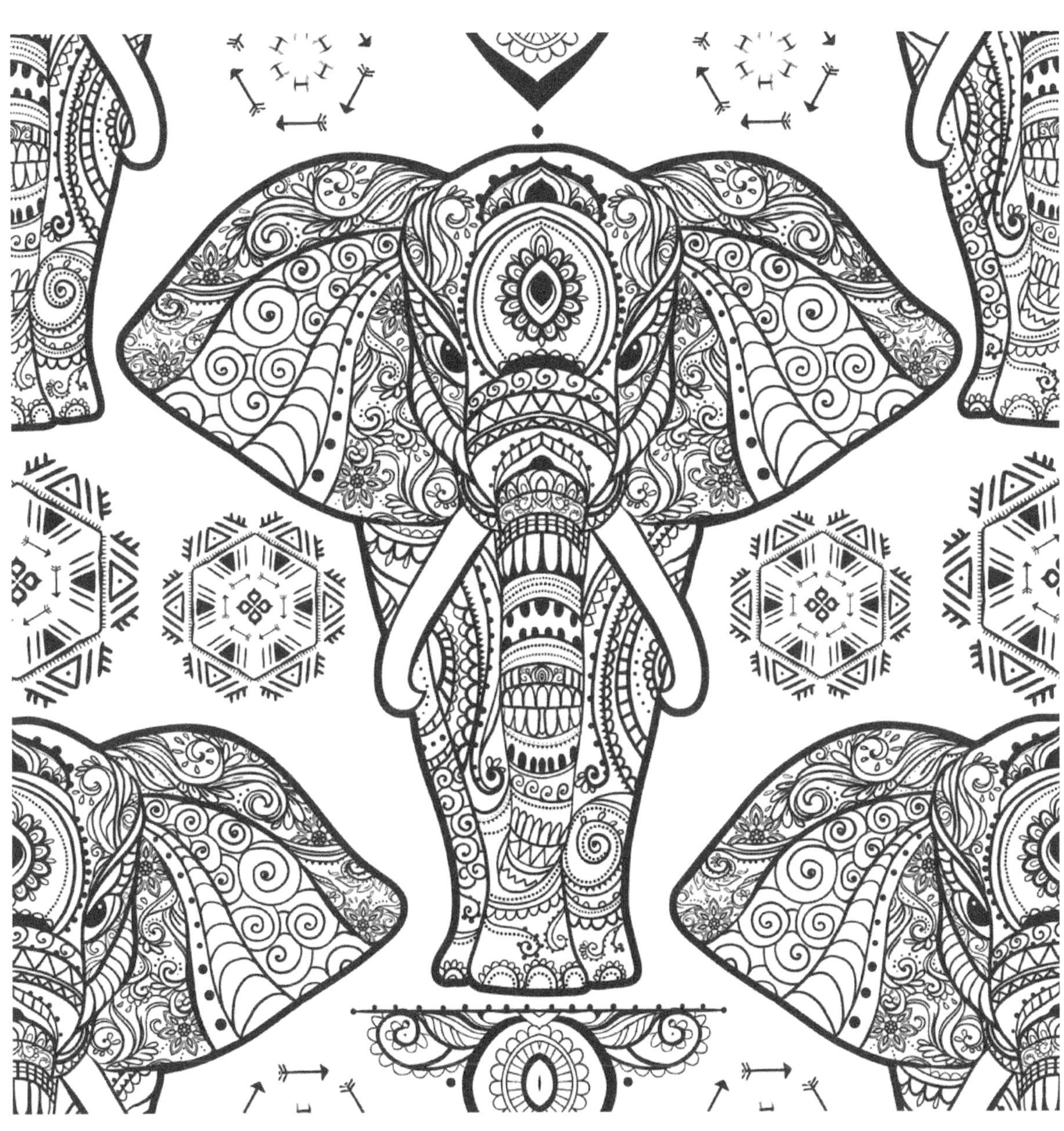

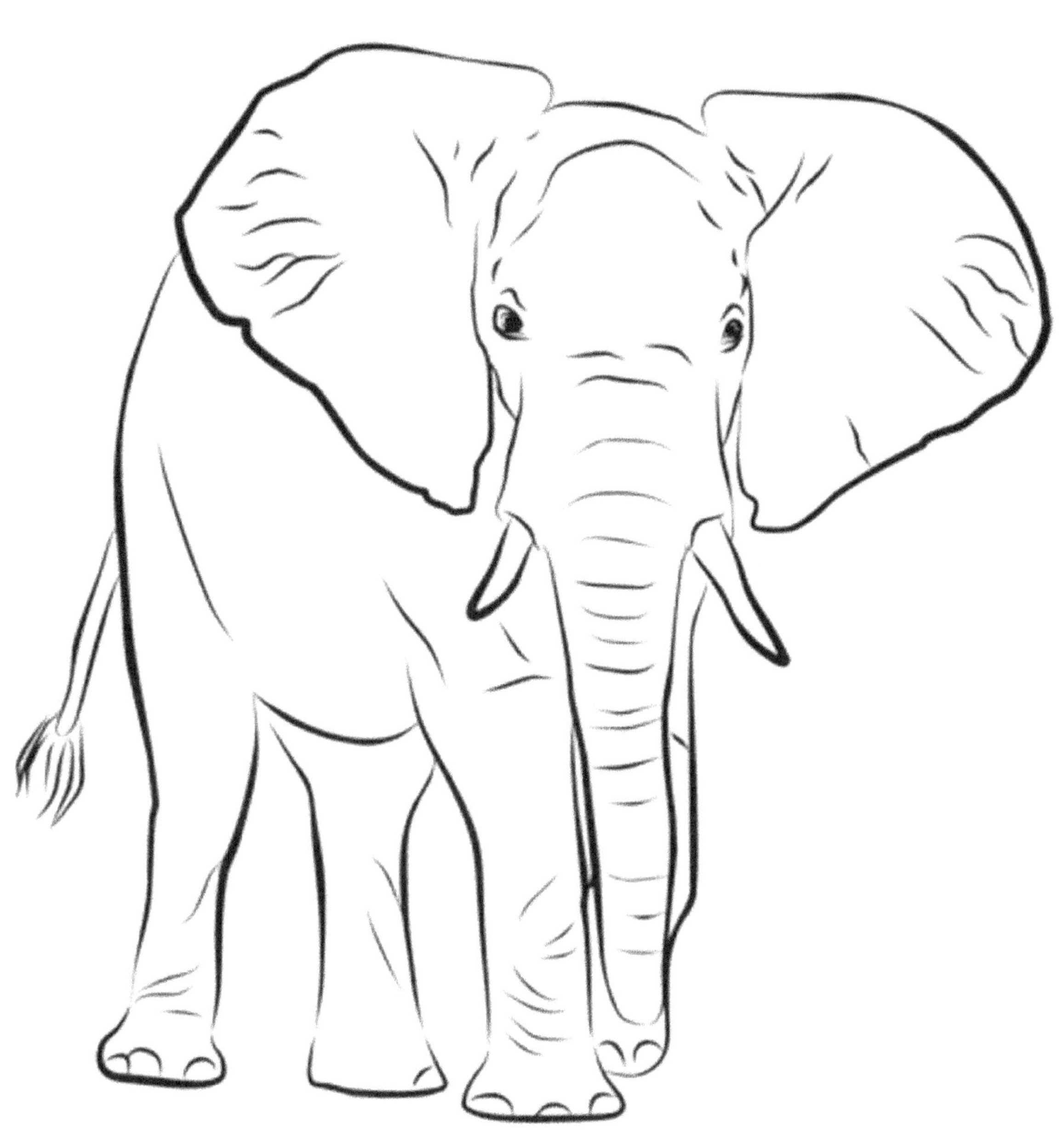

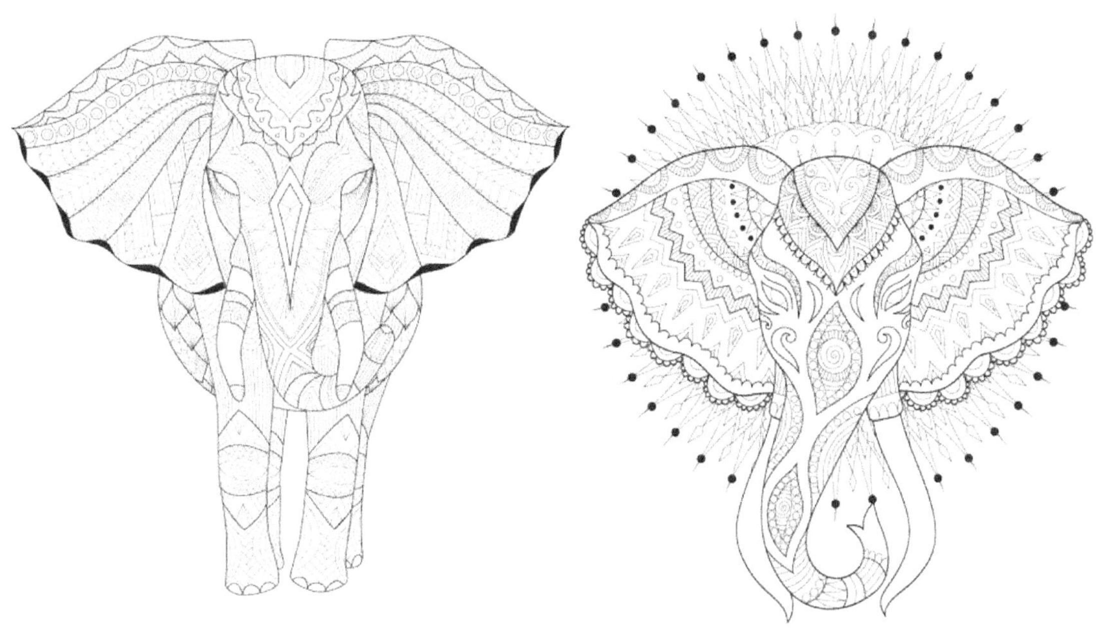

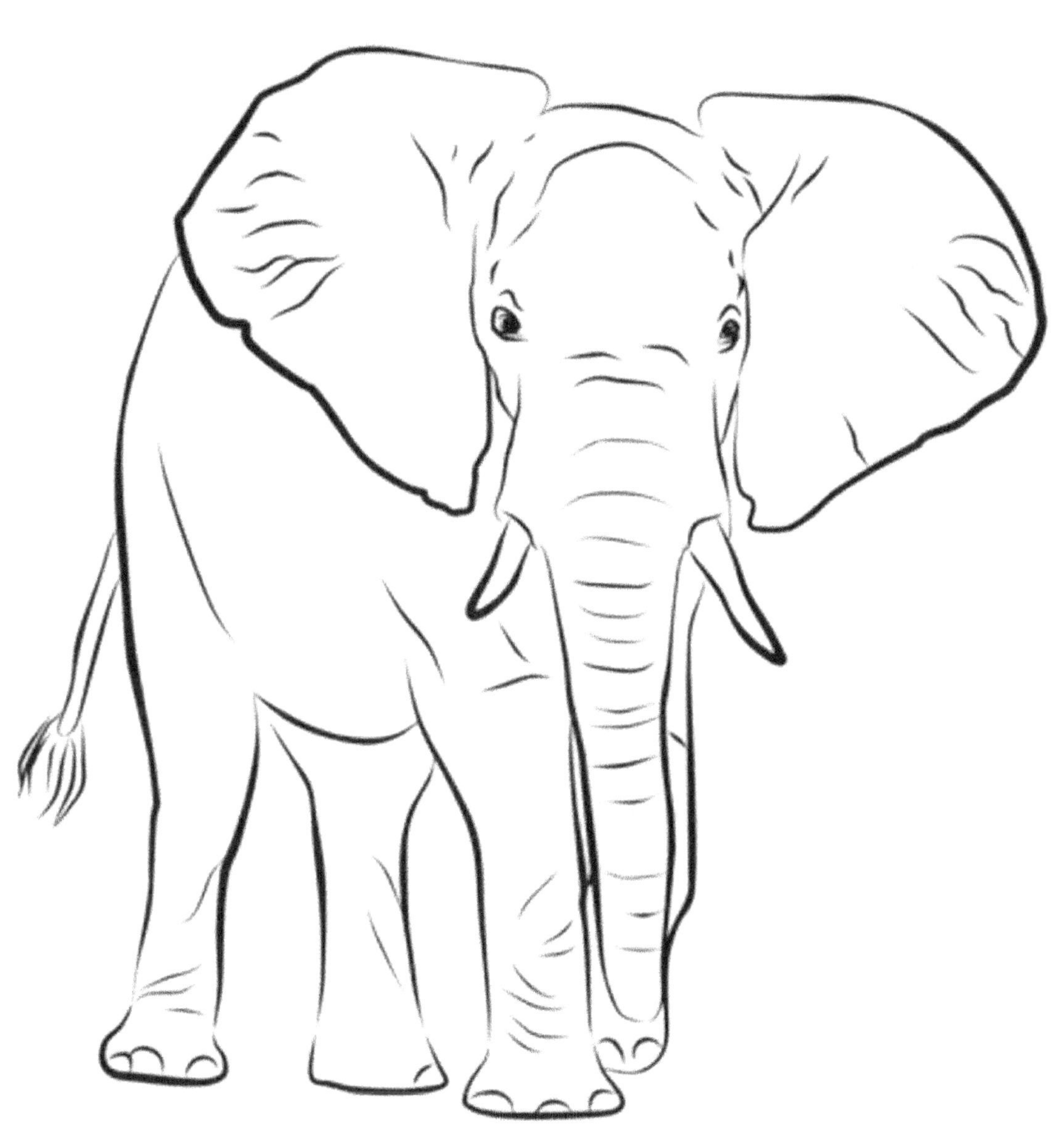

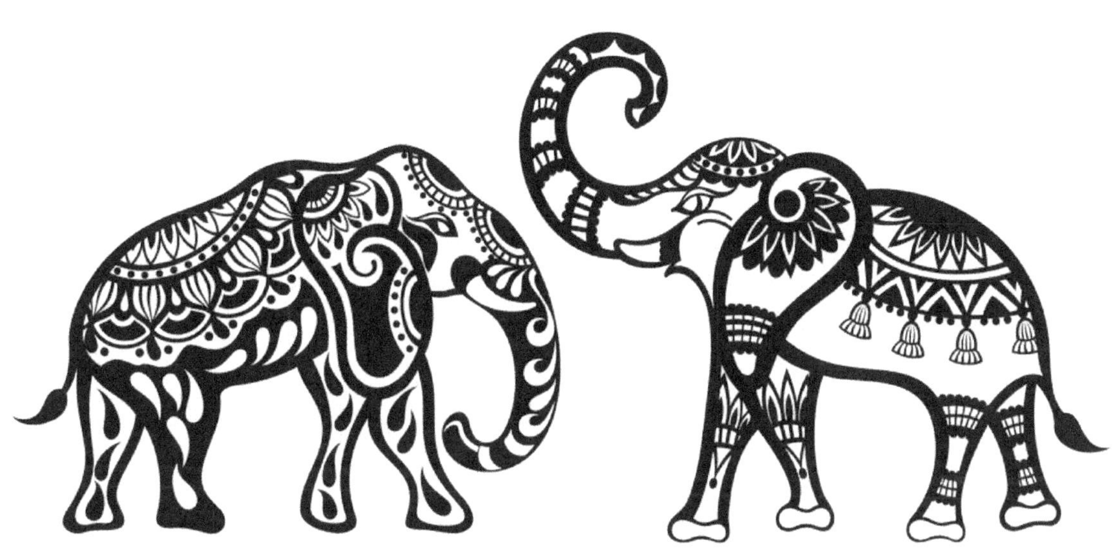

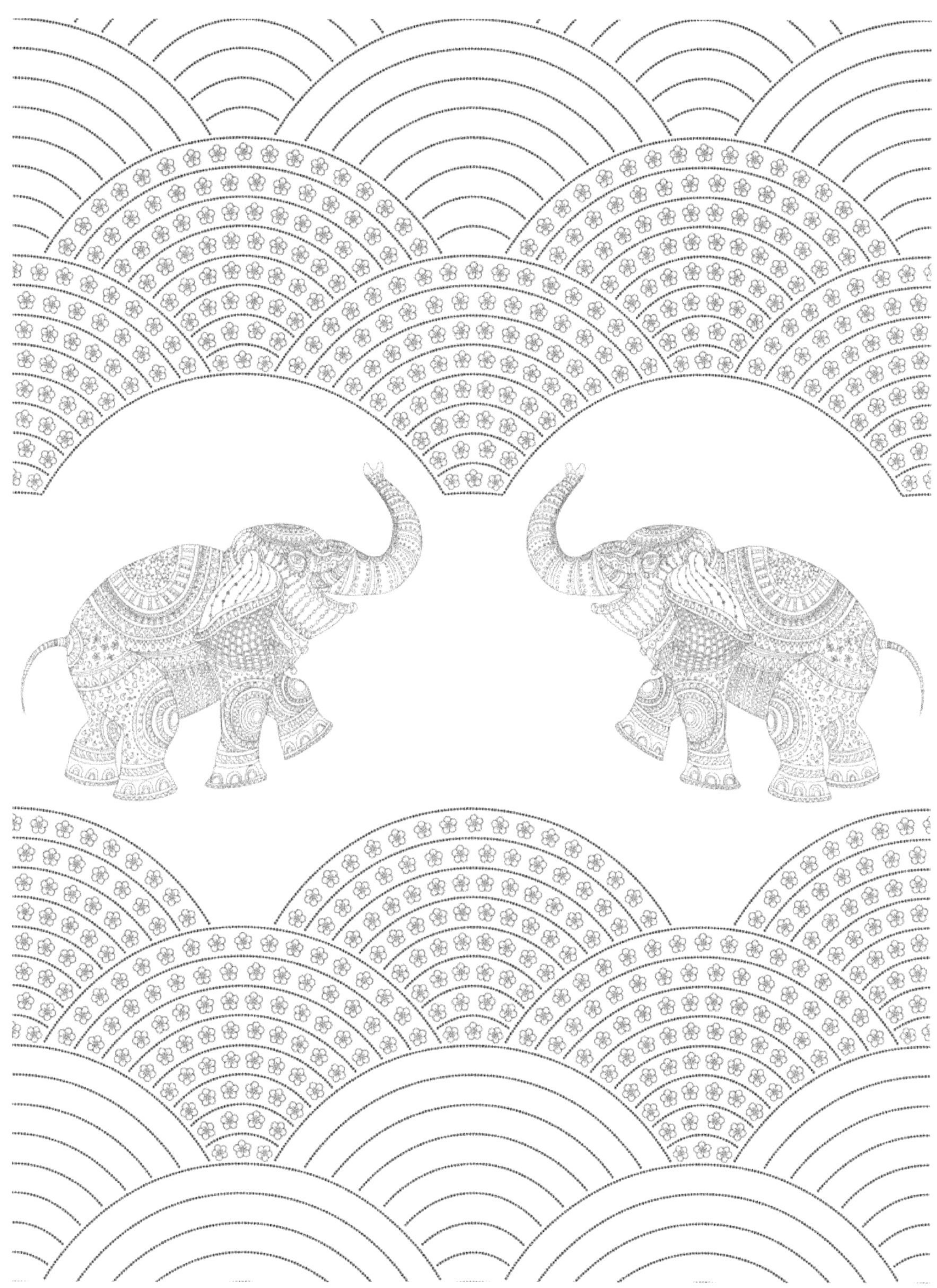

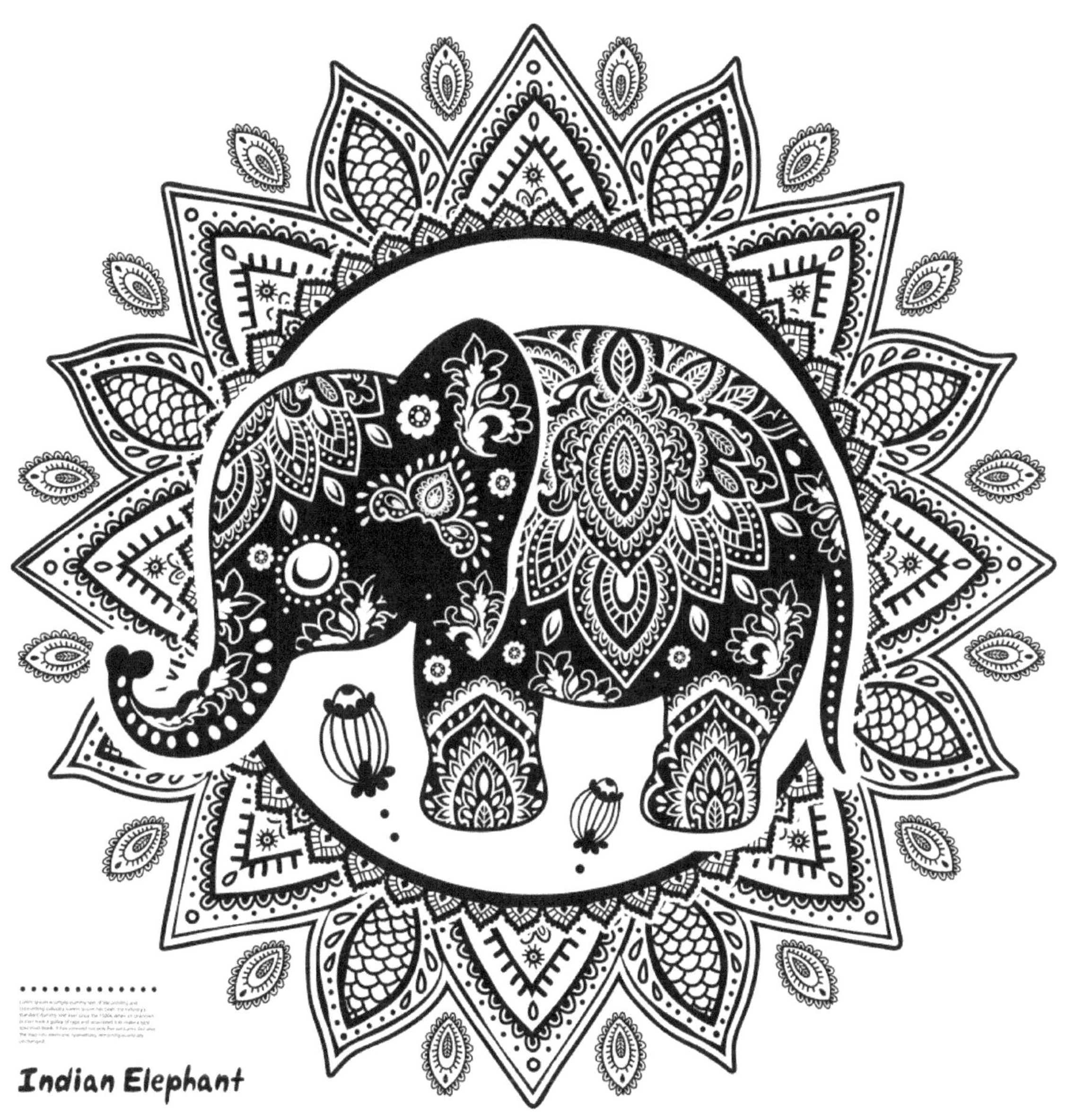

Indian Elephant

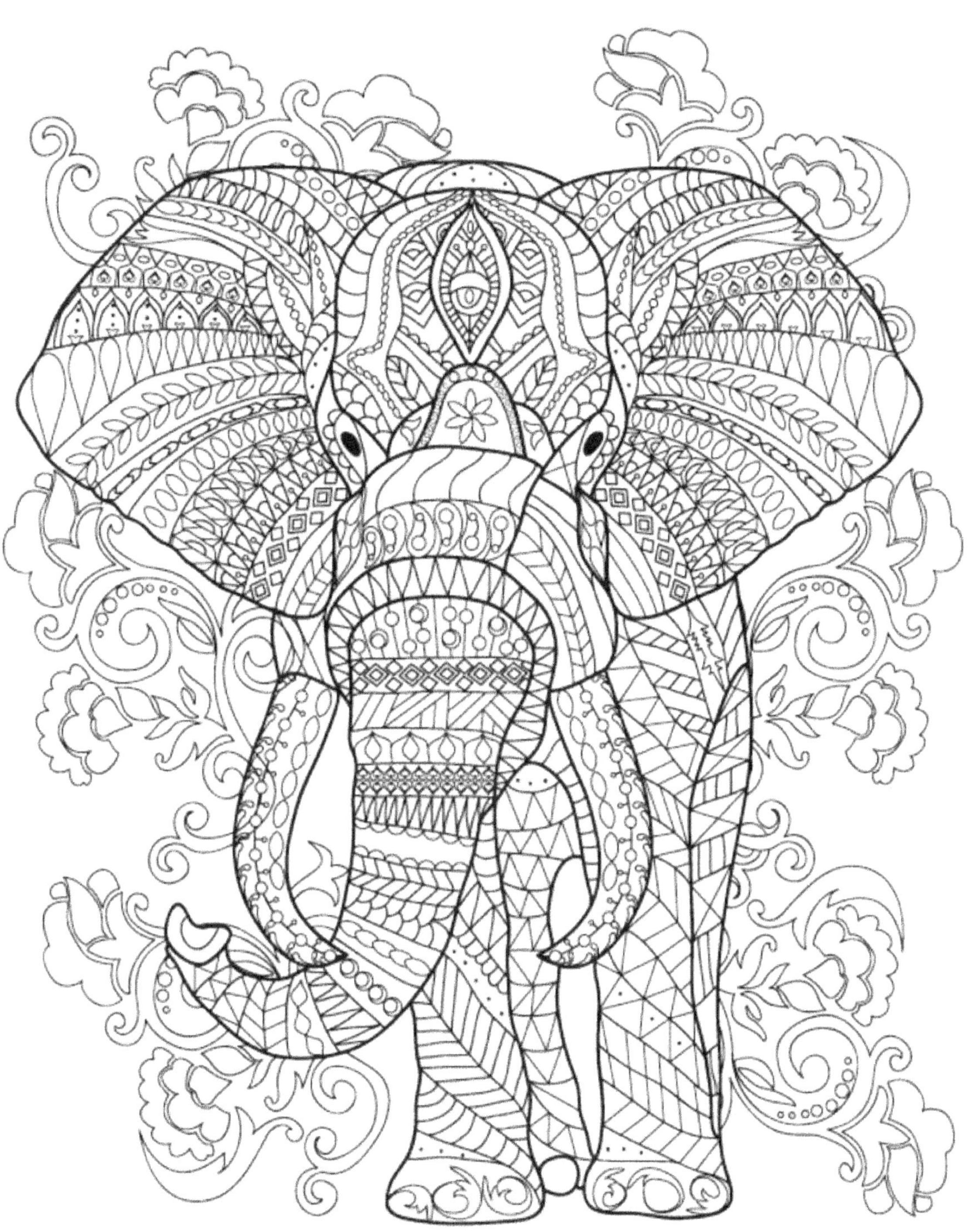

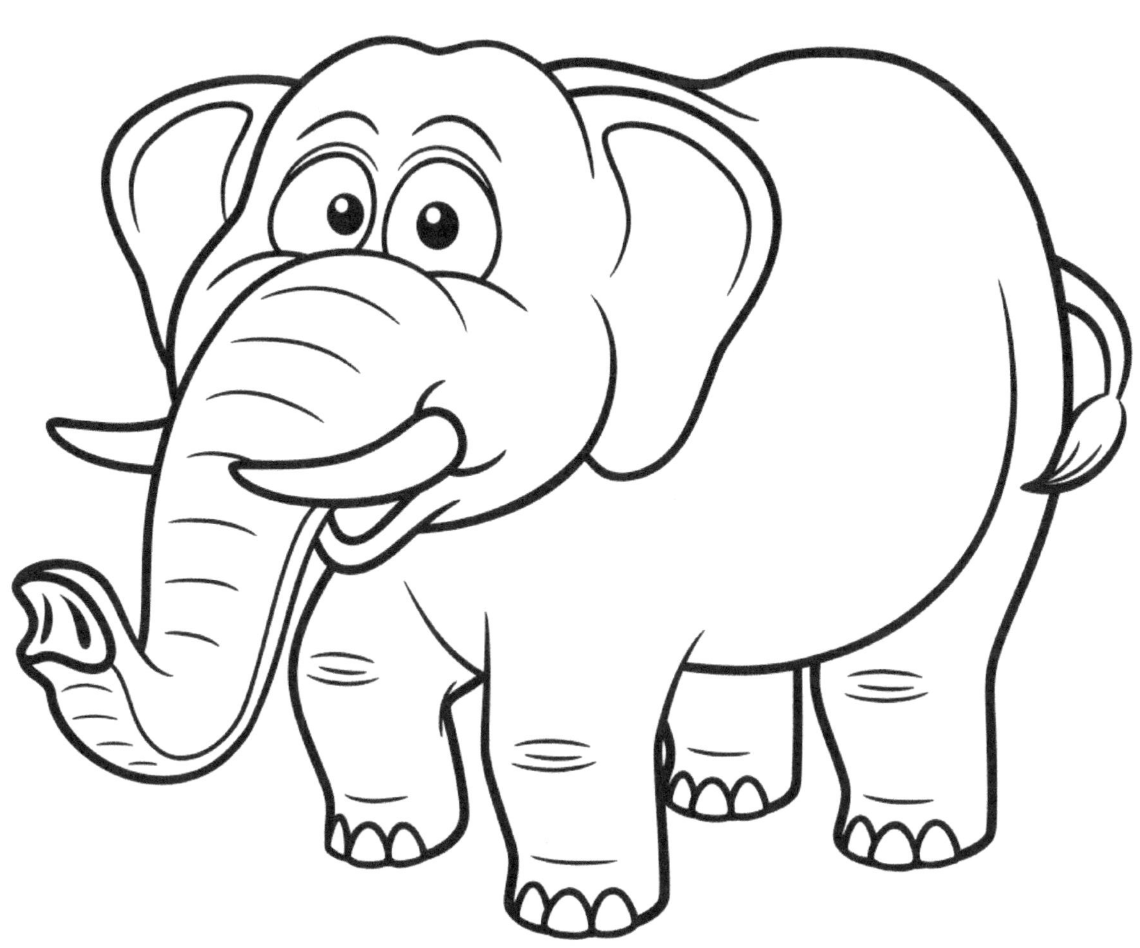

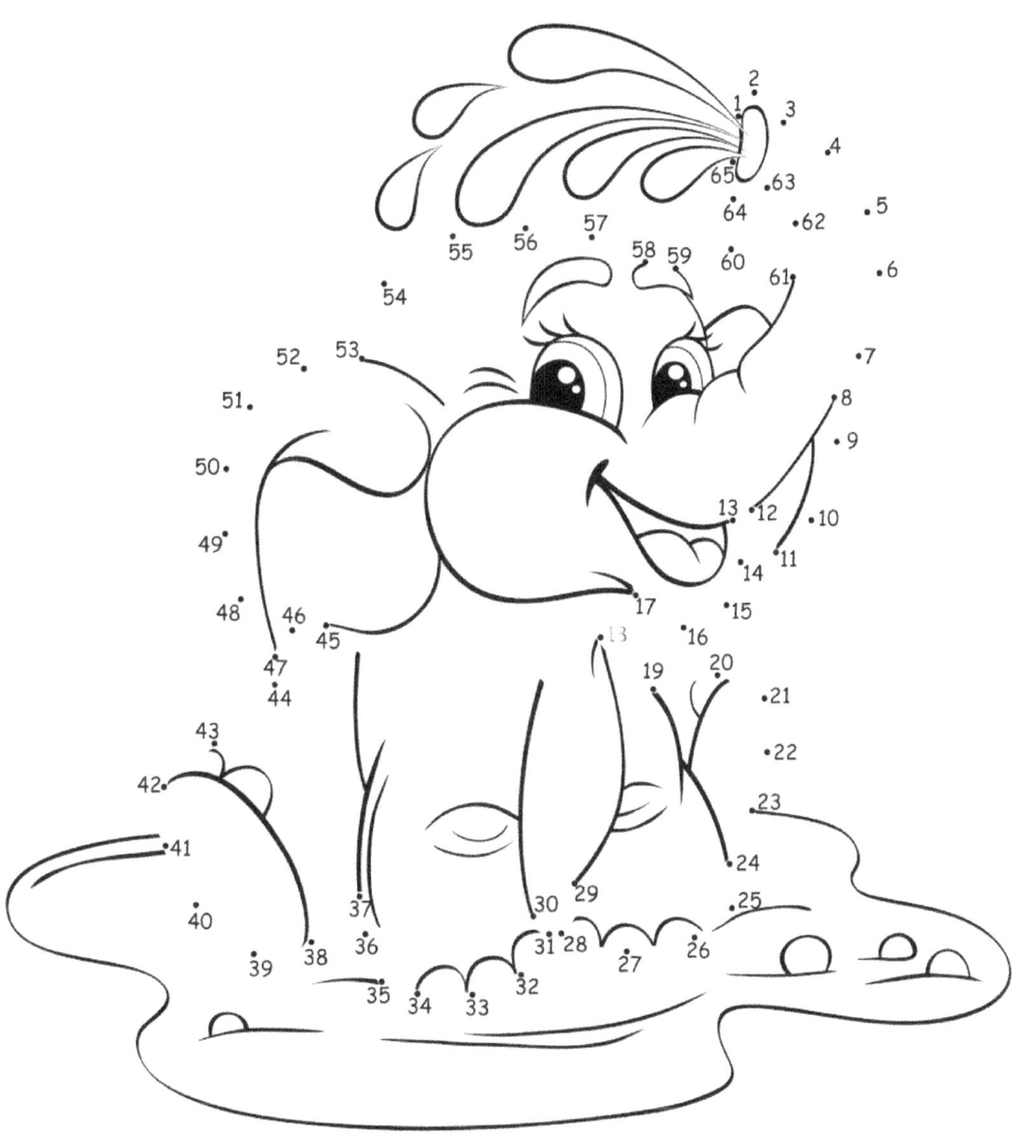

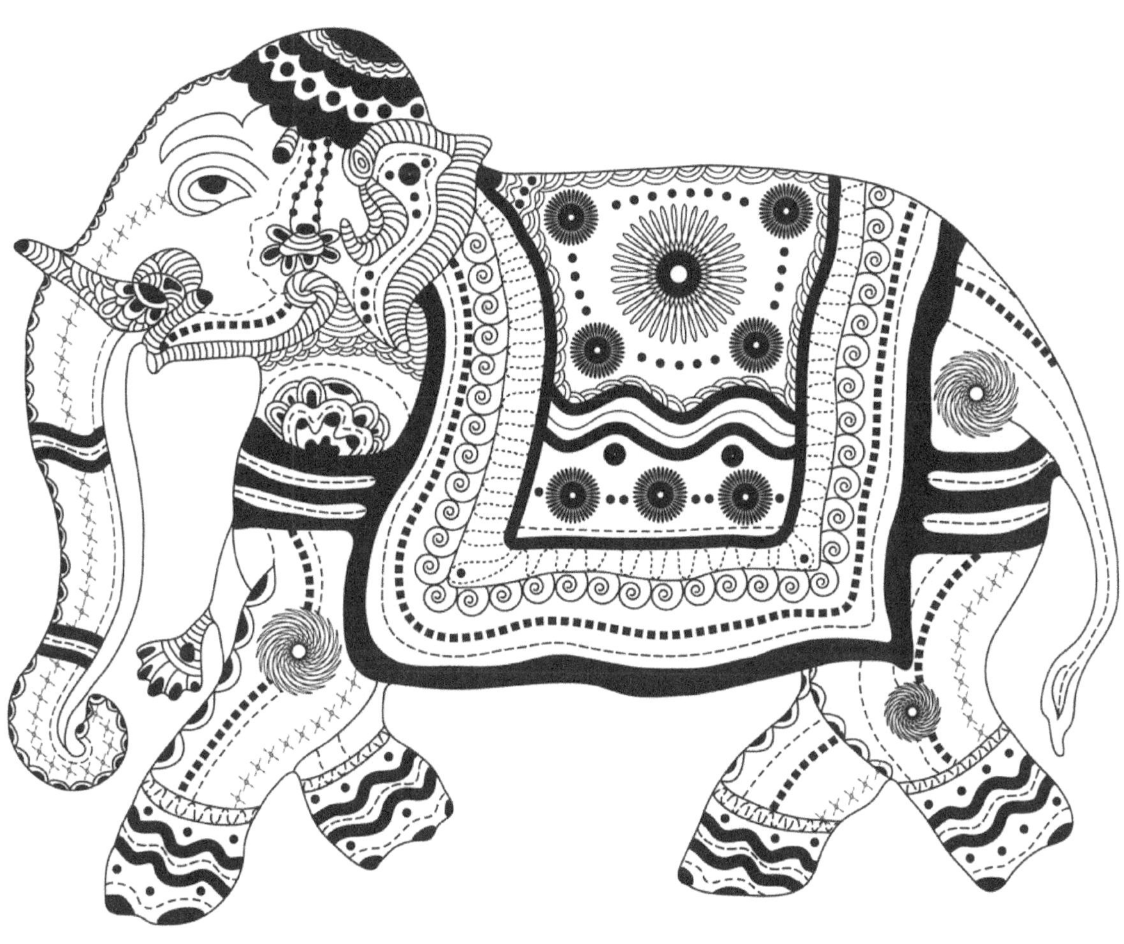

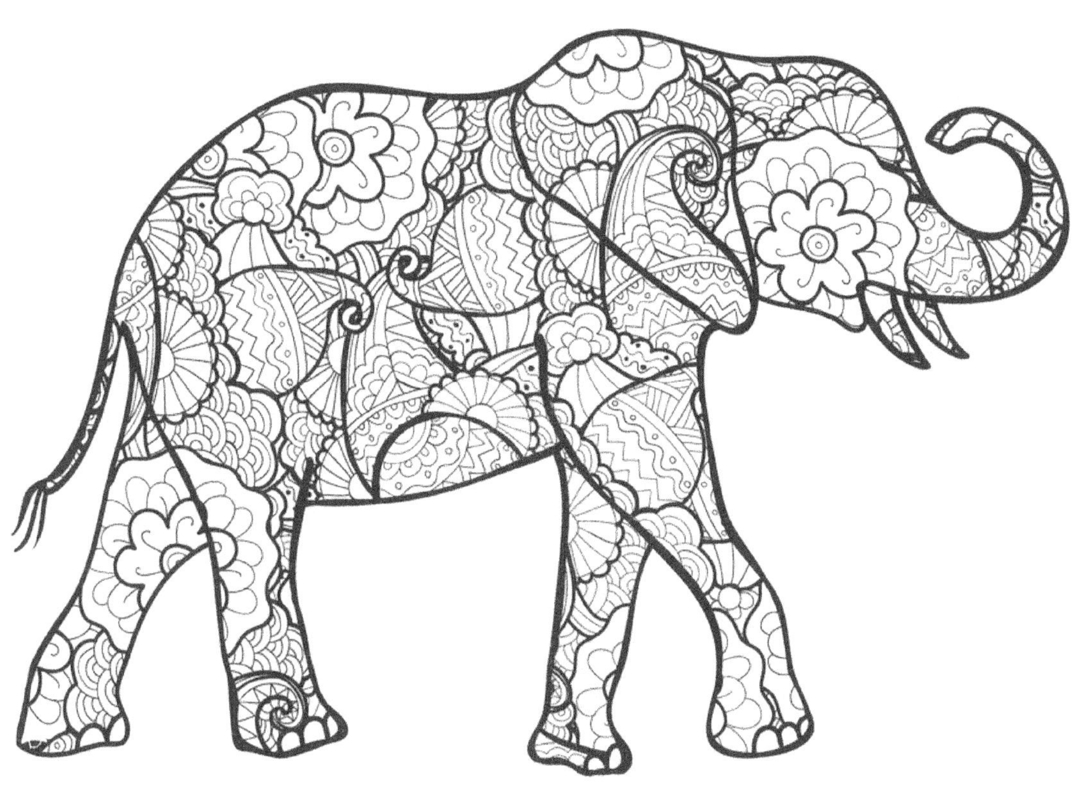

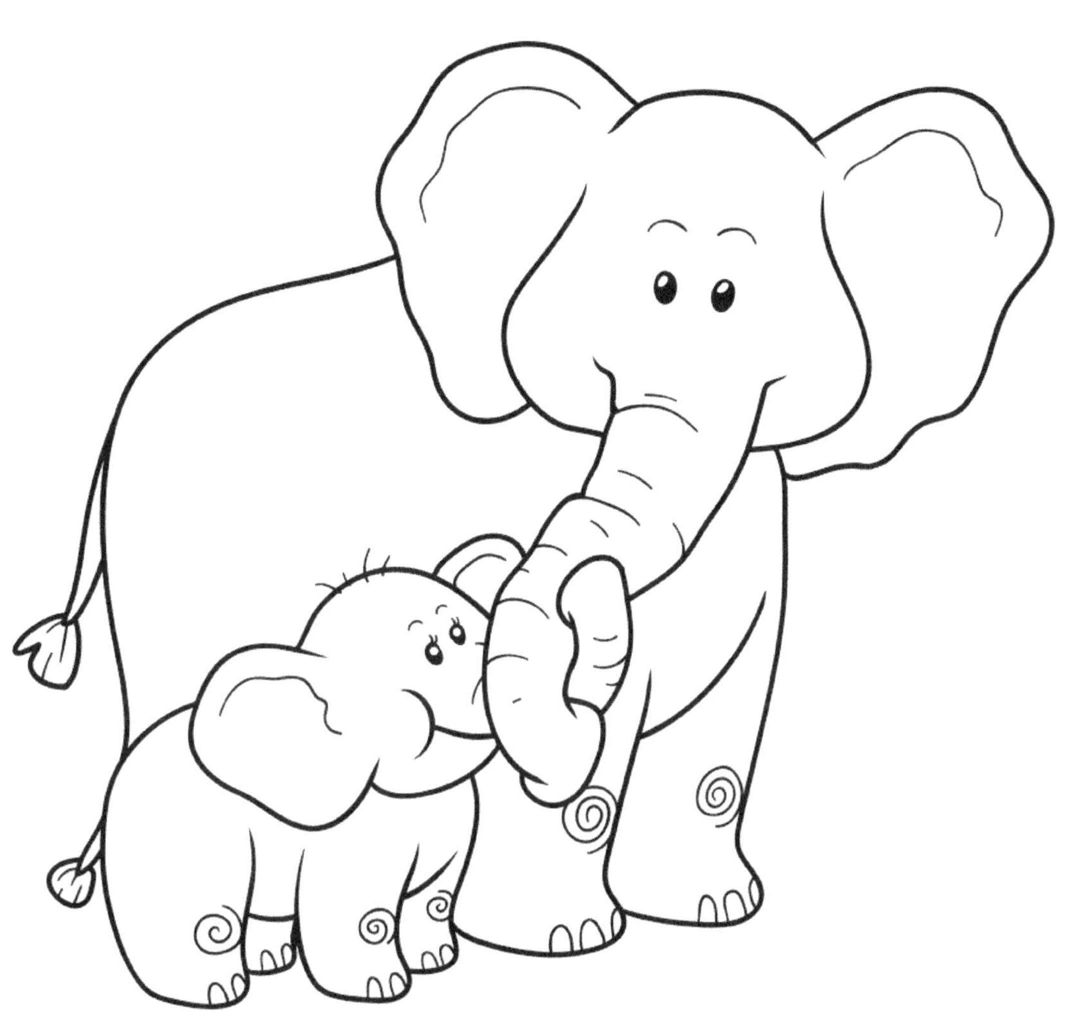